Jan. 17, 1997

CLASS ACTION

How to Create Accountability, Innovation, and Excellence in American Schools

CLASS ACTION

How to Create Accountability, Innovation, and Excellence in American Schools

John Katzman and Steven Hodas

VILLARD BOOKS   NEW YORK   1995

ISBN: 0-679-43430-5

Manufactured in the United States of America

98765432

First Edition

Dedication

Because education is about looking backward and forward at once, this book is dedicated to the cherished memory of Jim Zito, to the immanence of Emma Tilson Holland, and to the imminence of a new, improved Katzman.

CONTENTS

FOREWORD

This is a little book with some big ideas about an enormous subject—the future of American public education. Its goal is not comprehensiveness, because most people would find such a book to be nearly unreadable, and we intend for this book to be read. Nor does it attempt a scholarly review of the vast literature the field has generated, most of it similarly unreadable and much of the remainder hopelessly ideological.

Our project is more limited and, we feel, more productive. First, since the hateful features of all systems were conceived by their designers as solutions to an existing problem, we hope to provide a concise overview of the history of education as it bears on our current predicaments. Second, we'll put forth a framework that we think will better support debate and evaluation of new policies in such crucial areas as school administration, funding, and curriculum policy.

Our proposal is politically and pedagogically neutral. Rather than talk a lot about the content or distribution of education, we'll provide a means to appraise each of the many proposals that claim to improve our schools. At the same time, we believe our approach will lead to rapid advances in teacher professionalization, curricular innovation, and student outcomes.

This book is in part the product of an ongoing debate between the two of us, and our sense that the appropriate means and ends of public schooling are often far apart. During our work together, it became apparent that any tenable plan for reform was going to have to accommodate such divergence and dispute, that the failure of reform frequently derives from its tendency to impose the values of one group upon another. Despite what you may have heard, it is indeed possible to avoid this imposition while supporting excellent schools. More than anything else, this book is an attempt to sketch—in purposely broad strokes—what such a system would look like. We hope that the details will be filled in during a lively and wide–ranging public debate that would accompany implementation.

This book is also the result of the generous (and sometimes maddening) contributions of many colleagues, chief among them Mr. Jonathan Rowe. We'd also like to thank Betty Malen and Michael Knapp of the University of Washington for providing much of the ideational armature which gives this book such coherence as it does possess (although its limitations are purely our own). Thanks also to Meher Khambata, our resident magician, and her production staff. Finally, as critical and sympathetic editors, Catherine Holland, Alicia Ernst, Glenn Berkey, Kevin Campbell, Rod Pellett, Nick Lowenstein, Lewis Ernst, Lee Elliott, Cynthia Brantley, Maria Russo, John Weiss, John and Mark McWeeny, Jen Overbeck, Jennifer Nicholas, Patricia Krebs, Jenny Robbins, Andy Lutz, Ken Adelman, and Julie Katzman tightened much of our argument and spared you our excesses.

INTRODUCTION

How Did We Get Here?

It's easy to find fault with how schools are structured, what they're teaching, and how they're teaching it. Each era has had its own complaints, solutions, and experiments. Today's discontent finds expression in catchphrases like "school choice," "charter schools," "vouchers," "national curricula" and "national standards." Although they represent a range of approaches and ideologies, all these proposals—and most others that have captured the public imagination—have one thing in common: They're doomed to fail because they don't examine our educational system from a historical perspective.

Before anything about our schools can be changed for the better, we have to answer some questions. Why are our schools structured the way they are? Why do we continue to use error-filled textbooks that are much less interesting than almost everything written about almost anything else? Why do we have curricula that are remarkably the same from school to school even in the absence of a national curriculum? It will be difficult to structure a better system without first understanding the answers to these questions and others that are equally fundamental.

Many of the problems with our schools have their roots in the long-running debate over local versus central control. On the one hand, you probably don't want some bureaucrat in Washington deciding what your school teaches. On the other hand, you would like to know whether your schools are doing as good a job as are schools in other places, which means being able to judge all of them against some common standard. Any sensible proposal for reform has to take this conflict into account.

Guerrilla Reform

During the course of our research, we grappled with countless curriculum reform proposals, each one leading us closer and closer to an inevitable conclusion: No matter how good our ideas may be, they have almost no chance of being broadly adopted if we stick to conventional methods, channels, and processes. Real educational reform is something frequently talked about, but rarely enacted.

That's not to say that nothing changes. Content changes, especially, are always with us: "New math" drives out "old math" and is in turn superseded; reading instruction goes back and forth between phonics and whole language; curricula designed to be "relevant" or multicultural come and go. But the fundamental way schools work, their "look and feel," remains essentially unchanged from the model designed to serve a workforce that was either agricultural (the reason schools close in the summer) or early industrial (the reason schools have bells and class periods). In fact, despite all the educational debates and fads of the past thirty years, the American educational system has remained so static that a teacher from 1964 could probably dust off her lesson plans and walk into today's classroom, and no one would know the difference.

We're Not Angry

Relax. This is not another book about how pathetic our schools are, or about the ignorance of American kids. We're not going to relate a lot of anecdotes about a handful of great (or terrible) teachers we've found in our travels. And we're not going to argue that everything would be fine if we all paid higher taxes, fired all of our teachers or administrators, or privatized the public schools. The situation in which we find our schools is too complex for simple answers.

American schools aren't actually all that bad. They're probably as good as they ever were, and they're probably as good as any other country's schools. Our kids aren't stupid or ignorant (even the Generation X kids who've lived through disco, rap, and Beavis and Butt-Head). But our society—our democratic culture as well as our changing economic base—needs more from our education system than it did one hundred years ago, and it needs different things. We need schools that evolve and that innovate constantly, and that learn from each other's experience. Today's schools learn almost nothing from each other or from society (most are happy using equipment and management structures that businesses have already thrown out). We need schools that inspire confidence in students and parents, if for no other reason than that their complete lack of accountability makes people loathe to spend money on them, producing teachers and administrators who are poorly paid and demoralized. The crisis of confidence in schools' ability to manage themselves leads to a spiral of ever more testing and ever less teaching, of declining productivity within an increasingly expensive environment.

As we've struggled to find an acceptable solution to all these problems, we have used as a springboard an insight shared by everyone familiar with college admissions: The real customers of schools are not parents and students but colleges and businesses. If a school's students find work, or get into good colleges, that school is understood by most people to be doing a good job.

What We Won't Discuss

There are problems with American schools we will not directly address in this book. We have views on the crucial issue of school funding, for example, but it's a huge subject that deserves its own book. We talk a lot about curricula, but do not address what we think students should actually be taught. (Should high school students be taught history, math, English, a foreign language, sex ed, computer programming, and science? How much of each? What's most important?) We're not claiming to know what principals should be doing, or what fourth graders should be taught, or the optimal class size for high-school chemistry. Teachers know best how to teach. Principals know best how to administrate. We're merely proposing a system by which they, and others, can experiment to find out what works best for their kids, intelligently evaluate their work, and so improve upon it.

This book is not about school choice, either. As we've explored choice, we've realized that, whatever the merits of each of the various proposals currently circulating, the very notion of choice is meaningless—and perhaps dangerous—if there's no reliable way to judge schools before making choices, or if every school is forced to be identical to all the rest.

Although we don't address most of these issues directly, we believe that public discussion of all of them will be radically transformed for the better by the model we propose. To love our proposal, you don't have to accept any particular set of premises about what kids should be taught, how schools should be funded, or what level of choice should exist.

Debate over what schools should do and how they should do it will always be with us, which is as it should be. Our contribution, we hope, will be to help schools improve continuously and organically.

Multiple National Curricula

You're probably aware that the U.S. is turning to a national curriculum–the Goals 2000 program. For reasons we discuss in chapter four, such a program would be a disaster. How would we, as a country of 250 million people of wildly varied cultures, agree on one standard? And how would we update this standard and encourage innovation? The government is terrible at setting detailed performance specifications. By the time they have passed through the endless levels of review, horse–trading, and political scrutiny, the standards are obsolete. That's why the government's own technological infrastructure is always at least a generation behind that of the private sector.

What's needed is a system for schooling that combines what's positive about a national curriculum—its rigor and accountability—with flexibility, vitality, and local control over what and how subjects are taught.

What's needed is a wide variety of what we call "multiple national curricula." Under our plan, schools might choose from among fifty American-history curricula developed by public agencies, private companies, teachers, or community groups. Many of these curricula would probably be pretty similar to what's taught in most schools today, differing perhaps in their approach to assessment or their choice of source materials. Some, we hope, would be radically different, viewing our country through the lens of, say, its scientific or military or labor history.

Each of these curricula would include its own national assessment in the spring. Some might replace the classic final exam (essay or multiple-choice) with a portfolio or final project; perhaps some might be conducted entirely on-line with students from around the country. But whatever the specific methodology, each school would be held accountable for meeting the measurable goals of the curricula it chose.

The structure we propose for multiple national curricula in chapters five through eight supports diversity and innovation while enabling parents and educators to rigorously evaluate the educational merits of each approach. It offers them the freedom to choose as they see fit, and the opportunity—for the first time—to separate out educational merit from the moral, social, and political interests that factor so heavily into how we organize schools and teaching.

You Don't Need to Be Terrible to Get Better

The problem with our schools is not that they're awful, or not as good as they once were, or not as good as those in other countries. The problem is that the way teaching and learning are organized promotes uniformity over accountability, and deters innovation and excellence. The structure of schools no longer truly serves society, if indeed it ever did. It shields everyone—teachers, administrators, and students alike—from responsibility for learning, and fails to take advantage of the vast quantities of information about what works and what doesn't that classrooms generate every day. The pursuit of uniformity makes it difficult for schools or teachers to best utilize the tremendously powerful information systems that are evolving right now, and it causes us to spend vast amounts of money for things that improve neither student learning nor the conditions in our schools.

These habits of organization grow out of habits of thought, and habits of thought change over time. No one imagines that an educational system designed from scratch today would look at all like the one we've inherited. The organization of people, of processes, of society itself, that seemed sensible in the mid–nineteenth or even the mid–twentieth century simply doesn't make sense any longer. It is fundamentally out of step with nearly every premise of organization, production, personality, and human learning that we hold today. We have never expected such uniformity in our system of higher education—one of the reasons it is the finest in the world.

Here and Now

What makes us qualified to speak about these issues, anyway? Neither of us has ever been a school administrator, though Steven has taught in several high schools and has been an educational consultant for nearly a decade. We bring substantial experience from the boundary between private industry and schools. The Princeton Review—which John founded and runs, and where both of us have spent a great deal of time—works with more than 70,000 students a year (from several thousand high schools) in its courses , and another million a year through its books and software. It sends up to fifty of its teachers to every administration of every important national standardized test (the SAT, GMAT, etc.), which keeps us in touch with the way students and teachers approach tests and testing.

Many people have had axes to grind against the wheel of American schools. Many have tried to impose one ideological agenda or another on public schools, or to dismantle them entirely. Our goal is not to add to that, but help clear some of it away. We'll try to be concise but thorough, and answer questions and concerns you have. If you think we've glossed over something, are out of our minds, or have hit the nail on the head, you can reach us by e-mail at john@review.com or stevenh@review.com.

John Katzman & Steven Hodas

It's a Wonder I Can Think at All

CHAPTER 1

Becoming Number Two

Been There, Done That

For two thousand years, people have thought schools were doing a lousy job. Every generation laments that its youth are more poorly educated, more uncivilized than those in days past. Still, the past fifteen years in the United States have seen such an avalanche of criticism directed at schools, teachers, and students that it is now commonly accepted that American schools are failing not just their students, but the nation as well. In fact, a 1983 Carnegie Foundation report entitled *A Nation at Risk* declared that "if a foreign power had attempted to impose upon America the type of educational system we have today, we would consider it an act of war."

These criticisms have been taken up and given credence by politicians, academicians, and school administrators alike. Yet most data on the subject show that no such state of emergency exists. This is not the same as saying that we don't need our schools to work a lot better than they do, or that we don't need them to serve different goals than they have in the past. But before we can begin to look at how to best improve our schools, we need to look closely at the arguments that purport to show the system is failing, or else we will merely be tilting at windmills.

A Rising Tide of Mediocrity?

Complaints about the rapid and dangerous decline of American schools are familiar to us all: Kids are learning the wrong things. They're not learning anything. They're not learning as much as Japanese kids. Teachers are lazy, poorly taught, poorly supervised, too concerned with maintaining classroom order or not concerned enough. There's a shortage of scientists and mathematicians, professions suddenly elevated to the status of precious natural resources.

To add insult to injury, the critics continue, America spends more on its educational system than any other country in the world, pouring bushels full of money into what seems to be a black hole. So the problem, they say, must lie not in any lack of commitment or shortage of resources, but in a lack of will and wisdom on the part of students, teachers, and administrators.

Half the country thinks we should spend more on schools, but voters consistently reject increased funding (read: taxes) for schools. Some people want a national curriculum of "back to basics"; others want a multicultural emphasis.

What is going on? Are our schools really failing? If so, *whom* are they failing, and why? Can they be fixed? What should be done and who should do it? How did we get into this mess anyway?

This book proposes some basic structural changes to the huge, complex, and self-contradictory institution we call school, changes on the federal, state, and local levels. Before we can get to our proposals, we need to explain a few things about the current state of affairs, how the status quo has evolved, and who benefits from it. We want you to understand how a rethinking of a few of the basic assumptions we hold about schools can lead to tremendous change.

Each week, it seems, a new study claims that American kids are illiterate, that they know less than their parents, less than their counterparts in other countries, less than they should. A recent article by University of Arizona professor David Berliner examines these claims one at a time. Here we present a summary of his findings.[1]

"SAT Scores Are Declining Dramatically!"

We asked hundreds of admissions officers whether they thought SAT scores had increased, decreased, or stayed the same during the past twenty years. Every single one has said that scores have declined.

On the surface, they're right. Since 1975 there has been a 1.6 percent decrease in average SAT scores. That means that American kids answer three fewer questions correctly out of the 140 questions that make up the test.

But such a decline means nothing. If you compare the 1975 and 1990 SAT scores of students who were similar in terms of sex, class rank, and other demographic factors, you find that SAT scores have actually increased dramatically over that time, from 900 in 1975, to 915 in 1980, to 950 in 1985, and 960 in 1990. In *every demographic group*, SAT scores have risen since 1975. The overall decline is due to a smaller concentration of wealthy white males (who, as a group, score very well) taking the SAT, and an increased concentration of poor, minority, and female students (who, as groups, score poorly). This change in the mix of all test–takers has masked the large score rise within each group.

> Demographic shifts are also the reason behind the widely disparaged re–norming of SAT scores that goes into effect in the spring of 1995. The original mean of 500 on the math section and 500 on the verbal section was established decades ago to correspond to the SAT–taking population at the time. This group, wealthy white males, still scores about 1000, but it currently makes up a minority of test–takers. Since the composition of SAT–takers has changed dramatically, the new curves reflect today's population. This is not a "lowering of the bar" but rather a practice of honest statistics.

While no cause for celebration, the slight decline in average scores is certainly no occasion for hand-wringing. In the past twenty years, the number of disadvantaged kids taking the SAT has increased tremendously with minimal impact on scores. Generation X-ers, who are supposedly achieving less because of forced busing, lousy teachers, no homework, and permissive parents, have generally performed better on the SAT than their glorified predecessors.

"Results of standardized achievement testing demonstrate that kids know less than ever before!"

This statement is simply not true. The National Assessment of Educational Progress tests are given to a national sample of nine-, thirteen-, and seventeen-year olds in math, science, reading, writing, geography, and computer skills. Scientists at Sandia National Laboratories have analyzed this data and concluded that "the national data on student performance does not indicate a decline in any area," and concluded that "students today appear to be as well educated as previously educated students." This bombshell of a report, published by one of the nation's most respected scientific laboratories, was never widely reported in the press. In fact, it was voted one of 1993's "Ten Most Censored Stories" by a panel of media experts.[2]

One crucial piece of information is almost never acknowledged by the ax grinders when they construct their unfavorable comparisons between today's students and those of prior generations: The makers of all achievement tests revise their scoring procedures approximately every seven years in a process known as "re-norming." If, for example, a test is designed so that students score an average of 75, and over time, scores have crept up to 80, the testing company changes the curve so that the average is again 75.

On average, achievement tests are re-normed about three times in a generation. And despite what you may think, the curve is almost always made tougher. Armed with this knowledge and the students' scores on the tests, we can say with confidence that about 85 percent of public school kids today score higher on standardized achievement tests than did their parents. You may not like MTV, but there's no evidence it's dumbing-down your kids.

Yes, the SAT is an exception. As described above, that's because the population taking it has changed so dramatically over the past fifty years.

"Education used to be better!"

Some of the most unpleasant moments in the discourse on public education came in the second half of the 1980s when the American public was treated to barrages by E. D. Hirsch, Allan Bloom, William Bennett, Diane Ravitch, and Chester Finn on the subject of the dangerous and morally bankrupt empty-headedness of American teenagers.

Ravitch and Finn went so far as to construct and administer a test to substantiate their claims. These and other findings were quickly picked up as gospel and broadcast by the press, so that they came to be seen as self-evident.

A dubious claim like this becomes accepted to the degree that it strikes a chord with people's anxieties. Our favorite is the story of about the same time that single women over thirty had a greater chance of being murdered by terrorists than they did of getting married. Susan Faludi, writing in Backlash: The War Against American Women, illustrated how the spinster–terrorist victim myth was well received because it served a prevailing ideological climate.

Any test, of course, can prove whatever you want it to prove, depending on how you write, score, and interpret it. Dale Whittington, writing in the American Educational Research Journal, analyzed the test used by Ravitch and Finn to support their preconceptions in their 1987 book, *What Students Know.*[3] Whittington discovered that the test was composed of questions designed so that half the people answering a given question would get it right and half would get it wrong. In other words, an average, random student would score 50 percent. So far, so good. Then, Ravitch and Finn arbitrarily set 60 percent as a passing grade which meant that given the questions they used—more than half the people were guaranteed to be given a failing grade. In short, the test was rigged.

Whittington went on to make meaningful comparisons between what kids know and what their parents and grandparents knew at equivalent ages, something that those who claim schools are doing a lousy job seldom trouble themselves to do. Whittington tracked down the social studies and history achievement tests administered in this country since 1915. She compared the tests for content, difficulty, and demographics of test-takers, and was able to examine the performance across generations on the fields of knowledge that were common to all the tests.

Of the forty-three items on the Ravitch-Finn test that could be matched to questions on the older exams, Whittington found that today's students performed less well than their parents, grandparents, and great-grandparents on about one-third of the items, about the same as their ancestors on another third, and better than their elders on the remaining third. The answer to the whine of "What's the matter with kids today?" is, "Well, not much, really, at least when it comes to history and social studies knowledge." Which is not to say you can't make them look bad if you rig a test to prove a point.

In the restrained but precise language of an academic, Whittington concluded that

> . . . the perception of the decline in the "results" of American education is open to question. Indeed, given the reduced drop-out rate and less elitist composition of the 17-year-old student body today, one could argue that students today know more American history than did their age peers of the past.
>
> Advocates for reform in education and excellence in public schooling should refrain from harkening to a halcyon past (or allowing the perception of a halcyon past) to garner support for their views. Such action . . . is dishonest and unnecessary.

"We spend more on education than any other country!"

This is repeated by so many people who have the data to know better that one is forced to wonder why they say it. During the Reagan and Bush administrations, high-ranking officials repeatedly proclaimed that when it comes to education, the U.S.:

1) spends more than Germany and Japan;
2) spends twice as much as the Japanese;
3) spends more per pupil than most industrialized nations;
4) spends more per pupil than any industrialized nation.

None of these statements is really true, but just how false each one is depends on what you mean by "education." If you mean combined kindergarten through twelve, college, and university spending per capita, then the U.S. is in a three-way tie for second place with Canada and the Netherlands, behind Sweden. We achieve that rank because we send two to three times as many people to college per capita as most other countries. This is not the case if you're talking about K–12 spending alone, however, which was the topic before each of the "experts" who made these statements. When we adjust the data for differences in the size of our respective populations and look at the percentage of income spent on education, the U.S. ranks thirteenth out of sixteen of the industrialized nations, slightly ahead of Ireland and Australia, but behind (in order) Sweden, Austria, Switzerland, Norway, Belgium, Denmark, Japan, Canada, West Germany, France, the Netherlands, the United Kingdom, and Italy. In absolute dollars *per capita* we spend 14 percent less than Germany, 30 percent less than Japan, and 51 percent less than Switzerland. In his review of a summary of UNESCO data, Berliner concludes,

> If we were to come up to the average percentage of per capita income of the fifteen other industrialized nations, just to the average percentage expended per capita in those countries, not to the levels of those countries that spend the most, we would have to invest an additional $20 billion per year in K-12 education . . . .
>
> Given the expenditures on K-12 education, I can only conclude that our education president, George Bush, was not telling the truth when his lips were read and he was quoted as saying at the education summit of 1989 that the United States "lavishes unsurpassed resources on [our children's] school-

ing." Actually, he should have said we are among the most cost-efficient nations in the world, with an amazingly high level of productivity for the comparatively low level of investment that our society makes in K-12 education.

"American kids know less than kids overseas!"

The problem with statements like this is that since schooling is so different in different countries, it's almost always a comparison between apples and oranges.

As a matter of social as well as educational policy, the U.S. uses school differently than do other countries. We keep a great many of our kids through eleventh and twelfth grade, while in other countries, eleventh and twelfth graders are an elite, just as they were in this country prior to World War II. Therefore, international comparisons of upperclassmen are by definition pitting our average kids against their stars. For instance, in the International Assessment of Education, the performance of the top 9 percent of students in West Germany was compared with 75 percent of all American students. Guess who won.

Just as important is the fact that we have a different notion of how kids should spend their time. American kids watch more TV, play more sports, socialize, and work for pay much more often than do their counterparts overseas. It's true that Americans spend less time studying than Europeans or Japanese, but it's not because they're lazy. It's because they live in a culture that tells them that these other parts of their lives are at least as important as school.

One last kind of foolishness about these comparisons should be exposed. It's pretty obvious to most people that kids can't learn what they haven't been taught. In other words, it doesn't make sense for me to test your knowledge of al-

Americans are not the only people who like to prove that their kids have become ignoramuses. A recent study by Reader's Digest *in England gave a nineteen-question test of basic history, geography, math, and current affairs to 501 teenagers. None of the respondents got all the questions right, and only two answered at least seventeen questions correctly. Ten percent could not find the British Isles on a map, 32 percent could not find Canada, and 46 percent could not find New Zealand. While only 48 percent of the students could name the year that World War II ended, the study took pains to point out that 98 percent knew the legal drinking age. Professor David Regan, head of politics at Nottingham University and a member of the National Curriculum Council said, "Whatever else youngsters may have acquired, facts and hard knowledge do not appear to be high on the list." Former British Education Secretary Kenneth Baker, in words that should be familiar to anyone who follows the cant that surrounds most discussion of education in this country, was quoted as saying, "Unless we make our young people as skilled and as well educated as those of our competitor nations we can say goodbye to much of a future for Britain."*

gebra unless you've actually studied algebra. Since the U.S. doesn't have a national curriculum, not all our eighth graders take algebra. So if you were to take a random sampling of eighth graders and compare it with a sample of, say, Japanese eighth graders, all of whom take algebra and take it at the same time, the results would be pretty predictable: You would expect that the Japanese kids would know more algebra. Yet when the Second International Mathematics Study did just this, and found that the average American student who did not take algebra knew less of it than the average Japanese student who *had* studied it, people took this as a symptom of American decline rather than a foolish comparison. Not surprisingly, these same critics failed to note that American kids who had studied algebra performed as well or better than their Japanese counterparts.

When comparisons are fair, and not constructed to prove a pre-existing political or ideological point, the evidence shows that American kids successfully learn what we attempt to teach them, that they learn as well as they ever have, and that they learn as well as kids in other countries. And they manage to do so even though they are more numerous, more diverse, and live in far more dangerous and impoverished environments (as represented by rates of homicide, malnutrition, and children living in poverty) than do their counterparts in other times and places. Given the relatively low level of commitment our society makes to education and to children in general—in terms of dollars and social priority, not rhetoric—our kids and teachers do a commendable job.

Kids who are supposed to benefit from being tracked into less academic programs seldom opt for it on their own. David Nasaw explored this phenomenon historically in *Schooled to Order*. He reports that around the turn of this century, when working–class students—"the children of the plain people," as a contemporary report put it—began to enter high schools in significant numbers, the National Association of Manufacturers pressured the schools into offering newly-developed vocational curricula to these kids. The "plain children" and their working-class parents had other ideas though, and overwhelmingly chose academic subjects. A decade earlier, when the high schools were almost exclusively middle-class, the percentage of students taking Latin was around 35 percent. As enrollment expanded to include the working class, enrollment in Latin soared to 50 percent of students. Algebra enrollments increased from 45 percent to 58 percent, geometry enrollments from 21 percent to 28 percent over this same period.

So What's the Problem?

If things are just fine, why worry about school reform? Because, simply put: We can do better. In fact, a whole lot better. Schools consistently fail to challenge students and teachers to their full potential; the average home-schooled child accomplishes in two hours what takes six in a classroom. The typical computer game is more dense with information than the average school day. A half-hour of music video teaches more about the world. Kids leave school ill-prepared for the requirements of modern entry-level jobs. The working conditions within schools—from the physical dangers posed by violence and decaying buildings to the regimentation and lack of autonomy encountered by teachers in even well-equipped classrooms—drive the most talented away from teaching. Poor kids are tracked into vocational, "business education," or special ed programs regardless of their goals or needs.

Up to 40 percent of the money we spend to educate our children is spent on administrative overhead that never benefits them. The money that does reach the classroom is often allocated inefficiently and inequitably, with the schools that need the greatest amounts of support receiving the least amount of aid. During the past decade, dozens of states and districts have gone to court to defend the property tax–based distribution of money to schools, and more than twenty have been found to be so egregiously unfair as to be unconstitutional. Across states, 1991 expenditures range from Utah's $2,800 for each of its 1,300,000 students, to New York's $7,600 on each of its 20,000,000 students, to the District of Columbia's $9,028 per student for 720,000 kids. This gamut obscures an even greater range within states: In New Jersey the city of Camden spent an average of $3,538 on each student in 1989 while Princeton spent more than twice as much, $7,725. In 1987, New York City spent about $5,600 per student while Manhasset, on suburban Long Island, spent $11,373.[4]

> Most private-sector companies keep their indirect labor cost (e.g., administrative staff) at under 15 percent of revenues. In our large school systems, this number sometimes exceeds 30 percent. Much of this expense goes to administer state– and federally–mandated programs to help disadvantaged and handicapped kids, and to provide the array of social services that schools now dispense. But much is also waste and redundancy.

The United States is among the very few industrialized nations that spends less on the education of its poor than on its rich. As a consequence, perhaps, we have the highest rates of imprisonment of any country other than South Africa, and, according to the United Nations, nine out of every ten children murdered in the industrialized world are killed in the United States.[5]

An Old Dog

The question of how much money we spend only begs the question of how well we spend it. The majority of research conducted during the past twenty-five years fails to show any correlation between higher spending and improved academic performance, at least as researchers have been

> *One of the biggest problems with measuring how students do is agreeing what outcomes are important and how to measure them. Academic achievement seems worth measuring, for instance. But are standardized test scores the best way to measure it? (They're the most common indicators.) Maybe high school graduation or college admission rates would be better, or essay-writing ability or number of books read per year. Depending upon what you think is the main purpose of school you might think starting salary, lifetime earnings, voter registration, or teen pregnancy rates are better ways to judge whether schools are doing what we ask of them.*

able to measure it. Simply spending more money on schools is unlikely—except in the most extreme cases of underfunding—to ensure better education.

In 1989 Eric Hanushek reviewed research that attempted to find a link between school spending and student performance.[6] He looked at 534 studies which explored the connection between spending to improve the teacher/pupil ratio, teacher education, teacher salaries, facilities, administration, and student performance. Of these, only 123 of the 534 found any effect that was greater than random chance. Of the 123 that were statistically significant, 63 of them—more than half—found effects that went in the *opposite* direction of what you'd expect; i.e. greater spending on teachers or decreased class size caused performance to decline. In short, once the data were adjusted to correct for population differences like socio-economic status and level of parent's education—known predictors of students' educational attainment—nearly nine out of ten studies could find no relationship between increased spending and increased performance.

> *Most studies appear to demonstrate that within a very broad range (between ten and thirty students), class size has little if any relationship to student performance. It has a very strong relationship, though, to levels of teacher satisfaction and stress. This is just one of many examples of the need to recognize the targets at which we aim with reform policies.*

This does not mean that it makes no difference whether we spend more or less money to educate kids, however. You need to look closely at the premises and assumptions of each study and not just take its conclusions for granted. For instance, kids who are the most difficult to educate are often put into smaller classes, which would skew the results to make it seem as if small classes don't support high achievement. Studies on facilities expenditure often use the age of the building as an indicator, but an old building could be a converted mansion and a new one a trailer in a parking lot. Since teachers with the same credentials and seniority are paid the same regardless of how well their kids do, spending more for higher teacher salaries across the board won't necessarily produce better teaching. Education statistics of the kind reported regularly in the news media should seldom, if ever, be trusted without further investigation.

Without reliable, broad-based data from which to draw conclusions, the answer to the question "How should we spend our money for schools?" can never be satisfactorily answered. That's one of the reasons we've developed our proposal. At the same time, a concern with measurable performance and real results shouldn't blind us to other considerations that determine how we spend money on schools. There are plenty of reasons that have nothing to do with test scores for wanting all our kids to go to safe schools with enough pencils, chairs, and working toilets. It is simply wrong to ask teachers and children to spend their days under conditions that most of us would reject out of hand in our own workplaces.

Who Put the Blue in Blue Collar?

Most people judge schools not against such abstractions as equity or intellectual attainment but by how well they serve society's stated and unstated purposes. In the nineteenth century, when our system of public education was developed, society's purpose for schools was essentially the production of assembly line workers who would take instruction and not talk back (more on this in the next chapter).

Today, the number of high school graduates who go directly into unskilled labor is low and dropping. For one thing, nearly half of all high school graduates undergo some type of post-secondary schooling. For another, those unskilled factory jobs have been disappearing at a rapid rate for some time now. Society has changed dramatically, but schools have not, and much of our sense of school failure reflects how out of step they are with our other institutions.

For instance, the organization of schools is still indistinguishable from the mills and factories on which they were modeled in the nineteenth century. More than one hundred years later, schools still echo to the bells of an industrial clock while following an agricultural calendar. Workers (teachers) take orders from supervisors (principals) who follow the dictates of boards of directors (school boards). Vocational schools (colleges of education) offer training of the narrowest sort, and teachers, rather than practicing a profession, mostly read sets of instructions out of shop manuals (textbooks). While modern workplaces have learned the value of active collaboration between management and those on the front lines, teachers' engagement with their supervisors primarily takes the form of union bargaining with an adversarial management over inflexible work rules.

There have been periodic efforts at bringing the content of the curriculum (as opposed to its organization) more into line with the modern world, most notably in the early sixties and seventies, but the look and feel of public schooling has remained essentially unchanged for one hundred and fifty years. We've examined and updated our factories, our infrastructures, our Constitution, even our military, but schools remain the same. It's not that they're failing: on the contrary, they're doing exactly the job they were set up and refined to do. It's just that we want them to do a different job now, produce different kinds of students and citizens, and we get angry when the old dogs can't learn new tricks.

Making Schools the Same . . .

Although most middle-class Americans are happy with their own schools, they tend to feel that something is not right with the system as a whole. When looking at schools overall they see a system that is too uniform in its programs while being undependable in its quality, and that resists or evades accountability. Even though each state is free to set whatever graduation requirements it likes, the economics and politics of textbook production and adoption and the prevalence of national standardized tests like the SAT impose a de facto national curriculum on schools. Given that there are more than 15,000 school districts in the United States, no national curriculum and no national teacher certification policies, it's remarkable that almost every biology class is so like every other one. Given that each state is theoretically free to award diplomas as they wish, how did it come to be that very nearly all high school classes in the academic subjects meet for fifty minutes a day, four or five days a week for thirty-six weeks?

The development and marketing efforts of the textbook publishers exert a strong homogenizing influence on what goes on in schools. The same goes for state mandates on the number of courses students must complete, how many hours those courses must be, the number of days in an official school year, and, in some states or districts, which textbooks must be used. Much of the remaining potential for idiosyncrasy in education, for its handcrafting as opposed to its mass production, is subdued by the ever more stringent and standardized certification requirements imposed on prospective teachers.

The drive toward stricter teacher certification requirements has been motivated by two forces. Policy-makers believed that putting prospective teachers through a uniform training program would reduce the variability of what goes on in the classroom. It's unnerving to some that "when the classroom door closes, the teacher becomes the curriculum," so they've sought to produce teachers who would, as much as possible, think and act predictably in the classroom. Ironically, teachers' unions have, by and large, supported such measures, believing that they enhance the status of teachers as professionals (see chapter nine), even though study after study demonstrates that these practices, rather than lousy pay or working conditions, are what keep the best and the brightest *out* of teaching.

The similarities in our class structures, our textbooks, and our teachers, the artifacts that most signify "school" to us, are passed on from generation to generation with little examination of whether they make much sense. They might or might not, but under the present regime of school governance no one can know for sure.

... Yet Somehow Different

Despite this unimaginative sameness, there are tremendous disparities in both teacher and student performance. While a great deal of student performance variation can be attributed to socioeconomic factors beyond the direct control of schools, much also stems from the haphazard nature of the ways we organize teaching. Teachers aren't trained or rewarded to keep up with research on what works in the classroom and what doesn't. The evidence they do have tends to be anecdotal and mostly derived from their own classroom. Even if they were able to keep up with current research, the studies coming out of universities on educational effectiveness are often contradictory and almost always open to serious challenge. Since schools of education are populated by professors who frequently have little contact with high schools—and even less regard for the practitioners who staff them—most of their research is retrospective: it looks backward from a particular outcome and tries to figure out what was responsible for causing it, rather than experimental in design. As we saw with studies on school spending, it's too easy to poke holes in this kind of research.

The performance of kids from around the world on the First International Mathematics Test was strongly correlated with such factors as mean percentage of children living in single-parent families and mean percentage of children who work. It was correlated almost perfectly—.99— with percentage of children living in poverty, and the U.S. has the highest percentage of children living in poverty of all countries included in the study.

The irony of this situation is that teachers learn a great deal from what they do every day. But without something to compare their experience against there is no way for them or anyone else to tell which particular elements in the complex, rich, and messy tangle of exchanges that take place in the classroom are responsible for a particular outcome. Did changing the order of the lessons make a difference? Was it the extra field trips, the collaborative projects, or the new computers? It's difficult for teachers to hook up with other teachers who taught the same topic in the same way and whose students were comparable in order to determine just which factors were responsible for the difference in outcomes. Just as they're not trained to evaluate studies performed by others, teachers are ill-prepared to design their own.

Somewhere in this country is the single best history teacher. Somewhere is the best math teacher, and the best English teacher. We have no way of knowing who those people are, or of properly rewarding them, or of making sure that other teachers and students will learn from them. When those extraordinary teachers retire, all their expertise will be gone and new teachers will start pretty much from scratch. What a waste.

How did such a system come to be?

C H A P T E R 2

How Schools Got This Way

Satan Made Our Schools

In some places in this country, public education is older than the country itself. Massachusetts, for instance, passed the world's first school legislation in 1647. It required all towns of a certain size to establish a school to help ward off the influence of "that ould deluder, Satan":

> It being one chiefe project of that ould deluder, Satan, to keepe men from the knowledge of the Scriptures, as in former times by keeping them in an unknowne tongue, so in these latter times by perswading from the use of tongues, that so as least the true sence and meaning of the originall might be clouded by false glosses of saint seeming deceivers, that learning may not be buried in the grave of our fathers in the church and commonwealth, the Lord assisting our endeavors—
>
> It is therefore ordered, that every towneship in this jurisdiction, after the Lord hath increased them to the number of 50 householders, shall then forthwith appoint one within their towne to teach all such children as shall resort to him to write and reade, whose wages shall be paid either by the parents or the masters of such children, or by the inhabitants in general—and it is further ordered, that where any towne shall increase to the number of 100 families or householders, they

> shall set up a grammar schoole, the master thereof being able
> to instruct youth so farr as they may be fitted for the univer-
> sity, provided, that if any towne neglect the performance
> hereof above one year, that every such town shall pay £5 to
> the next schoole till they shall perform this order.

This brief statute laid down the template for much of how we think about public education. It established the model of local control over the funding and staffing of a school for local children and took for granted that society had an interest in protecting itself from the proliferation of undisciplined minds: Intellectual development was only one of the jobs that school was to perform, perhaps not even the most important job. Fur-ther, it established our tradition that society's interest in education was greater than that of parents' right to choice in the matter.

These rules, and the values that drove them, did not spring up in a vacuum. Early New England schools, like most Puritan institutions, evolved out of a moral and religious concern with idleness, self-improve-ment, and community responsibility (Connecticut even passed laws in 1650 that took children away from parents who failed to educate them prop-erly). These themes were to play a big role in the way Americans thought about public education for the next 350 years. They were the template on which much of our system of public education was established, and they continue to provide a great deal of the moral force—and the rhetoric—of today's debate. One reason why proposals that emphasize the privatization of public education draw so much criticism is that they fly in the face of this centuries-old tradition. Curricular reforms that tamper with the fa-miliar classroom structures and lines of authority—originally established to instill moral virtue in impressionable young people—are viewed with similar skepticism.

Not all the colonies were as gung ho on schooling as New England. In other parts of the continent, some saw education as a threat to the existing arrangement of society. In 1671, the Governor of Virginia, William Berkely, wrote:

> I thank God that there are no free schools nor printing, and I
> hope we shall not have them these hundred years, for learn-
> ing has brought disobedience, and heresy, and sects into the
> world, and printing has divulged them, and libels against the
> best government"

What Berkely was paying tribute to—in a backhanded sort of way—is the potential for education to liberate minds as well as to discipline them. Tension between education as a liberating force and education as a means of channeling individual energies to serve the purposes of society has always existed. This is yet another aspect of the perpetual debate over the goals and purposes of public education.

While the Massachusetts School Law of 1647 may have required towns to set up primary schools, it didn't require children to attend them, and few did. It wasn't at all clear to most parents how formal education would help their children in a world made up of artisans, craftsmen, and small farmers. Until quite recently, not many families were wealthy enough to sacrifice their children's potential earnings to the luxury of education. As early as 1827, Massachusetts had passed another law, also widely ignored, requiring towns with more than 500 families to set up high schools to teach algebra, American history, surveying, bookkeeping, and geometry but, by 1860 there were only about 300 high schools in the entire country. Thirty years later, during the 1889-1890 school year, fewer than 7 percent of all fourteen to seventeen year olds were in school. It wasn't until child labor laws—the most significant pieces of "school legislation" ever passed—forced kids out of the workplace that high school attendance became the rule rather than the exception.

Revolting

Although we're used to rhetoric that emphasizes education's potential to open doors, the rise of public schools initially had a lot more to do with social control of "undesirable elements" than it did with providing expanded opportunity.

In the early days of our history, Americans and Europeans alike imagined that America would have no paupers, no beggars. America contained far more land than citizens, had no inherited caste system, and no legally enforced class boundaries. This seemed like a sure recipe for the material, social, and political independence of every citizen, on into the foreseeable future.

The coming of the industrial revolution, however, meant that goods were no longer made and sold by independent artisans and craftsmen who controlled the terms and manner of their own work. Instead, people worked for wages in factories producing goods that, a generation before, they would have made themselves or bartered with a neighbor. Patterns of farming changed, too, from small plots intended to sustain a family or community to large farms taking advantage of the new machinery. Many family farmers and craftsmen quickly went broke in this environment and, newly poor, streamed into cities in search of wage labor.

Daniel Webster remarked in 1820 that public education, rather than being a frill or luxury dispensed by the privileged to the poor, was "a wise and liberal system of police, by which property, and life, and the peace of society are secured." The mob violence that exploded across mid-nineteenth-century cities like New York, Charlestown, Massachusetts, and St. Louis only seemed to prove Webster's foresight. In 1877, the U.S. Commissioner of Education urged wealthy industrialists that "Capital, therefore, should weigh the cost of the mob and the tramp against the cost of universal and sufficient education."[1]

As cities started to fill, the optimistic republicanism of the older established families was replaced by a more frightened, more defensive posture toward their fellow Americans. For the first time, the poor were regarded as a threat as well as a reproach. Since they had no stake in the order of things that had made them poor, and perhaps bore some understandable resentment, an increase in their numbers held particular dangers for the governing classes in a democratic society. A monarchy can simply repress its poor with physical force; in a democracy, the poor vote. When Andrew Jackson, a back country Indian fighter, won the presidency in 1828 and ended the fifty-year reign of the best families of Virginia and Massachusetts, the writing was clearly on the wall. Society would need to be "managed" if it was not to decline further, or worse, degenerate into Jacobin anarchy.

Schools or Prison

Throughout the nineteenth century, private societies and municipal organizations worked together to address the gentry's fear of large numbers of unregulated paupers. For the first time, they built schools, prisons, poorhouses, and asylums, paying particular attention to what they considered to be the special problems posed by young children. Childhood was seen as a crucible for personality, the time when a little influence—whether constructive or malign—would determine the character of the future adult.

Poverty and crime were regarded as the outgrowths of moral insufficiency. Given that assumption, it seemed obvious that—to avoid becoming criminals or malcontents—the children of the poor needed to be taught discipline and respect for authority. Public education was not originally conceived as an institution to serve all citizens regardless of their station, just as it was never imagined that the wealthy or the middle class would be interred in prisons or asylums. "Education" as a public institution was designed as a preventive reform school for children who by virtue of their poverty were assumed to be dangerously indifferent—or even hostile—to the interests of their betters; children who, today, would be called "at-risk." Universal schooling, which began with the Puritans as a moral impulse, had been transformed through social insecurity into a moralistic imperative.

> *Even today, many people cite violent crime as the reason we should improve our schools. In giving $500 million to various school-reform groups recently, Walter Annenberg said he was trying to "drop a bomb" on the problem of crime.*

It's therefore not quite right to say that schools today are failing because they do not teach students how to read, write, think, or calculate properly. That was not the primary purpose for which they were originally organized; as noted, they were built to contain or transform otherwise dangerous social elements. Until we restructure them to reflect different priorities, we cannot expect much improvement. As the old saying goes: Never try to teach a pig to dance; you will only waste your time and annoy the pig.

Factory Schools

By the 1830s, every major city had a network of "Free Schools" sponsored by its wealthiest citizens. Many of the schools were copied from the British "monitorial" system developed by Joseph Lancaster, an early educational entrepreneur who enrolled more than 30,000 students in his ninety-five schools before going bankrupt. According to David Nasaw in *Schooled to Order*,[2]

> The teacher sat far above his students and assistants on a raised stage. The assistants or monitors, themselves older, unpaid students, marched up and down the long rows of younger students conveying the instructions of the teacher and maintaining absolute order. Students and monitors were arranged hierarchically. Every day, every lesson, students were moved forward or backward according to their performance. Monitors were also ranked. The head monitor was the only one in direct communication with the teacher, while the assistant monitors were informed through the "head" of the commands of the teacher. Students were punished for

> "talking, inattention, out of seats; being disobedient or saucy
> to a monitor; moving after the bell rings for silence; stopping
> to play or making a noise in the street on going home from
> school; and staring at persons who may come into the room."

Most schools at the time had only one teacher, and Lancaster's model enabled the average enrollment to increase from under sixty to over one thousand students. More significantly, it established the framework of school hierarchy with which we're familiar today, where workers are rewarded with promotion up the ladder from teacher, to principal, to assistant superintendent, and finally, superintendent.

Schools with this sort of factory model were very attractive at the time. They were modern and so signaled progress. They could handle greater numbers of students with the same resources. They prepared the children of the working poor for their future lives as parts in a huge social-industrial machine. As the authors of the 1874 *Theory of Education in the United States of America* put it,

> Military precision is required in the maneuvering of classes.
> Great stress is laid on (1) punctuality, (2) regularity, (3) attention, and (4) silence, as habits necessary through life for successful combination with one's fellow-men in an industrial
> and commercial civilization.

William Harris, a U.S. Commissioner of Education, wrote that society required "conformity to the time of the train, to the starting of work in the manufactory. The pupil must have his lessons ready at the appointed time, must rise at the tap of the bell, move to the line, return; in short, go through all the evolutions with equal precision."

The state superintendent of California proposed that for truants, the state should establish "labor schools, school ships, industrial schools" so that such children could be taught "how to work." We may cringe at such straightforward pronouncements today, and imagine that they reflect obsolete values and goals, but, in fact, very little has changed in the ways schools operate. Most students are still expected to work quietly at their stations until the bell releases them. Teachers are still judged by their peers and superiors on how well they are able to "control" a class. And students are still taught that the primary function of school is to prepare them for the world of work.

Common Schools

The Free Schools, along with the "infant" and "charity" schools that also attempted to transform the poor into willing workers, failed. The poor avoided them, partly because of the unrelenting attitudes of dominance and contempt the schools conveyed toward their charges, and partly because of the strong stigma in the still-young republic against accepting charity of any kind. Mostly, they failed because there were no laws compelling school attendance, and because organized schooling was irrelevant for success in most endeavors. Only relatively well-off families could afford to sacrifice their children's wages by sending them to school and they attended private academies.

During the 1840s, a generation of school reformers came into prominence and attempted to revive and spread the model of the old New England common schools. These were supported by taxes and tuition, and were attended by a broad cross-section of their communities. Reformers like Horace Mann and Henry Barnard were among the most tireless and well known of those evangelizing for the establishment of common schools throughout the country. In the common schools, children of rich and poor alike would go through a shared character-building experience. Thus society would be protected "against the giant vices which now invade and torment it—against intemperance, avarice, war, slavery, bigotry, the woes of want and the wickedness of waste." Education would offer the poor a chance to lift themselves out of poverty.

Unfortunately, most Americans didn't share the reformers' enthusiasm for widespread education, particularly if it meant paying taxes to support it. Consequently, school buildings were crowded and dilapidated, lacked outhouses, and were staffed by incompetent and dissolute masters. Then as now, school reformers sought the financial and moral support of business leaders. Reformers made the argument that schools were the only institutions capable of providing business with a steady supply of responsible, productive workers. The economies of the northern states depended almost exclusively on wage labor, and so these arguments persuaded the major industrialists to become strong supporters of the common school movement. In the southern states, where not much had changed since Governor Berkely's remarks one hundred and fifty years earlier, a society composed almost exclusively of slaves and aristocrats made reformist arguments about a pool of willing workers irrelevant. Planters saw little need for common schools and made no move to support them.

The debate over the taxation required to support common schools was fierce. Many citizens and legislators felt it was unconstitutional for the state to appropriate an individual's private property to pay for a service he might never use (there was no income tax in those days). Between the 1830s and 1850s many states passed and then repealed and then passed again laws permitting or requiring local communities to collect taxes for public education. Not until 1874 did the state supreme court in Michigan determine that it was constitutional for taxes to be used to support public high schools.

> In March of 1994, Michigan became the first state to eliminate the use of local property taxes to fund schools. After years of court battles it was finally decided that it was simply too difficult, if not impossible, to fairly finance public schools primarily through local taxes.

The money raised in this manner was seldom enough to cover the full costs of running schools. Many continued to charge tuition, or "rates," to the families whose children attended them. In the past, municipalities had granted reductions or exemptions to those families who could not afford school rates. As cities and towns grew larger, the personal relationships and familiar acquaintances on which the informal scholarship system depended grew less common. Many poorer families fell through the cracks, effectively excluded from the schools they financed with their own hard-earned money.

> Although the rhetoric used to argue for publicly financed schools stressed their usage by the poor, taxes for high schools went disproportionately to support the education of the middle class and rich. In 1893, the NEA Committee of Ten expressed the function of the high school to be "to prepare for the duties of life that small proportion of all the children in the country whose parents are able to support them while they remain so long at school." Similarly today, while all citizens pay taxes to support public universities, it is generally the children of the well-off who attend them.

Public Schools

In an attempt to provide general access to education, most states passed laws to prevent public schools from charging tuition. Since local tax revenues were generally insufficient to meet expenses, many schools responded by cutting the length of the school year, by paying teachers less, and by refusing to provide books for their students.

For the quality and quantity of schooling to vary so widely seemed to violate the spirit behind a publicly funded school system. In order to insure minimum standards of schooling for everyone, states began to mandate, as they do today, the number of days in the school year, the length of the school day, the required subjects, and so on. At about the same time, states began to work on the other side of the equation, compelling attendance, usually through age fourteen. Massachusetts passed the first such law in 1852, and by 1900, thirty–one states had them. When first conceived by the Puritans two hundred years before, the common schools had been responsible solely to their local communities. With these new laws, which asserted the right of states to regulate the terms and conditions of the schooling in their towns, villages, and cities, state governments became a strong and vocal partner.

Still, local influences predominated, and schools took on the character of the immigrant communities they served. In Boston, boards fought successfully to remove textbooks that contained outrageous ethnic slurs against the Irish as a matter of course. In St. Louis and Cincinnati, public school boards demanded bilingual instructors to teach classes in German. Polish, Italian, Czech, Norwegian, and Dutch were introduced into elementary schools as options around the turn of the century. The great-grandparents of many of those who today resist the use of any language other than English in schools were likely to have been instructed in their own "foreign" tongues at public expense.

> *The profession of school-teaching was a common form of upward mobility for immigrants: In 1908, nearly 50 percent of all New York City teachers had foreign-born fathers, mostly Irish or German, and it has been estimated that as many as 75 percent of New York City public-school teachers in the 1930s and 1940s were Jewish women.*

Professionalization

At the turn of the twentieth century, control of municipal government—including schools—became increasingly split along party (and often ethnic) lines. This was met with resistance by the displaced Protestant elites who had held most of the control in the past. As the power and visibility of immigrants began to extend to the schools, there were more and more calls for "professionalization" and reform that would "take the politics out of schools." These challenges were widely understood by the citizens of the period—with much justification—as thinly veiled appeals to anti-immigrant and anti-Catholic feeling.

To say this is not to deny that many city schools were in need of reform and oversight, or that ward politics encouraged some of the most spectacular municipal corruption in American history. It reminds us, though, that battles over schools are never fought on neutral territory. They are always to a large extent battles over much broader social issues made more vivid and more urgent by their involvement with children. Similar battles are being fought today over "multicultural" education, as various factions struggle over the vision of society and the cultural values that will be transmitted to children by the state.

Corporate Urban Schools

Those who designed nineteenth–century urban schools regarded them as a sort of human factory. Since the classroom was the basic unit of production, its operation received most of the attention. By the turn of the twentieth century, classroom mechanics were largely well established, and design efforts shifted to the organization of classrooms in relation to one another. When thinking about how to organize individual schools into a school system, administrators looked again to the business world, this time borrowing the model of the corporation. This was not surprising, since corporate managers and directors often played key roles at the core of school reorganization efforts.

At the same time as this struggle for control of schools from the top down was underway, the Progressive ethic of "professionalization" and "expertise" began taking hold as a model for municipal government in general. This ethic attempted to reform schools from the ground up in the hopes of rooting out the endemic corruption that had plagued their management. These two currents of reform—top–down and bottom–up—joined together, frequently moving to replace the large number of fractious local boards and committees with a single, small, central board led by a powerful and distinguished superintendent—a cross between a university president and a corporate CEO. This central school board would house the necessary expertise and authority to make all decisions of consequence. In cities of any size, this meant a lessening of the power of the community to run their schools directly.

The makeup of such a board determined where its loyalties were and whom it would best serve. If schools were to be tools and institutions of their local communities, school boards would most appropriately retain a strong local character. If they were to be instruments of larger social policy, the boards would be responsible to people at higher levels. Since the goal of school reformers in this period was generally to limit local influence, they usually lobbied for appointment of board members by the governor. In practice, they often accepted a compromise of state-wide election of "at-large" members who represented no particular district. Since at–large members were not responsible to a particular community, they tended to be more receptive to the policy recommendations of the socially prominent and their sympathetic "experts." In short, the goal of the reformers was to ensure the control of school boards by the right sort of people.

Extensive publicity campaigns were conducted to convey the message that local boards were unfit to govern schools. Equally unfit, of course, were the residents of immigrant districts where, as one advocate of centralization put it, "There are vast throngs of foreigners where one scarcely hears a word of English spoken, where the mode of living is repugnant to every American."

Meanwhile, the newspapers and magazines of the period were evangelizing the successful, disinterested businessman as having a special aptitude for the management of public affairs. Professors of educational administration, a newly minted university department, were frequent speakers at public and private meetings intended to convince politicians and influential citizens that centralizing school governance was central to reform. In return, these professors received generous and prestigious consultancies to the reform committees.

> *The school historian David Tyack has shown that between 75 and 100 percent of those active in the movement to centralize school governance in Philadelphia were listed in either the Blue Book or the Social Register. So dedicated were the reformers to wresting control of the school from the people that they even questioned the universal franchise. In 1891 a committee of the National Education Association, a strong supporter of the centralization movement, recommended limiting the right to vote "by excluding the grossly ignorant and vicious classes."*

Who's in Charge?

The struggle over school governance reflected fundamentally different visions of how society should be ordered. On one side were the local school boards, the teachers and principals, the ward committees and political clubhouses, and the residents of ethnic enclaves who wanted schools to serve their particular communities rather than abstract notions like the public good. On the other side were both social progressives and frightened reactionaries who believed that schools should be instruments of social policy; that, as the means by which society re-creates itself, they ought to be brought into the modern world of centralization and specialization; and that running a school should be no different than running a corporation.

For more than one hundred years, the most popular means for changing how schools go

> *It was common for the wealthy supporters of board centralization to advocate that school board positions, as a sign of their importance to the public trust, be unpaid. This of course excluded from service those who needed a to be paid for their work in order to support their families.*

about their business has been to take power away from them and vest it at some higher level, like the district or state.

The idea here—sometimes hidden and sometimes openly stated—is that the closer an institution is to its community the less it will be able to perform competently and honestly. This impulse has its roots in the urban corruption scandals of the nineteenth century, and in the frantic, xenophobic efforts of the gentry to hold on to its social influence as society changed around it.

As we'll see, the solutions devised over a hundred years ago by the centralizers, whatever their motives, remain the template for school organization today, and are the greatest obstacles to meaningful change.

Defining the Boards

Different states resolved the battle for control in different ways. Some created extremely strong central positions for statewide school superintendents or boards. Some eliminated local boards altogether. Other states, particularly in the West, held on to their traditions of strong grass-roots control of education and maintained authority in local community boards. In general, the composition of a state's school board can tell us how centralized a state's education system is. At one extreme are those boards elected by and representing local districts, and at the other are boards appointed by the governor to serve at-large. Of the fifty chief state school officers, eighteen are elected, twenty-seven are appointed by state boards, and five are appointed by governors. Thus, thirty-two out of fifty—nearly two-thirds—serve without direct public accountability.

Where local boards exist, they are generally authorized to establish schools, employ a superintendent, make rules and policy, and raise and expend money. There is a limit to these powers, however, since they ultimately derive from the state; the boards remain bound by what state law sets out for them. In addition, the resources and procedures with which school boards operate are often outside their control and relatively unchanging. For instance, most school districts depend on local property-tax valuation for a majority of their financing. These rates are in turn set by assessment boards and county- or state-determined formulae over which school boards exert little or no direct influence.

Local school boards jealously guard the authority they exercise, in part because it is a source of significant political and economic power. They oppose school-choice measures, for example, in large part because allowing kids to attend schools outside their own districts lessens the board's power. As middle-men between the state and the schools, they generally resist plans that allow schools to have greater freedom to govern and manage themselves, as well as plans that allow states to set standards and impose restructuring. The 15,000 school boards with their 97,000 members, are a powerful political force, complete with a lobbying organization that is among the most active in every state.

> The National School Boards Association (NSBA) has taken official positions against teacher professionalization (because of the expected increase in salaries it would bring), as well as against increased parent and teacher involvement in the governance of schools. In New York, the SBA is the third largest state lobby, following New York City and the Hospital Association of New York State.

The continuing power of these local boards can be viewed as a sign that the early centralizers failed in their attempt to concentrate power outside the communities. On the other hand, the boards' composition, which is disproportionately white, male, and wealthy even in ethnic and blue-collar communities, can be read as an indication of their success. Nationally, school board members are 65 percent male, 97 percent white, and 38 percent of the members have annual incomes in excess of $70,000.

Going by the Boards

In some cities, like New York, local board posts are high-paying and highly politicized, and have tremendous significance in the broader arena of city and even state politics. When New York City school chancellor Raymon C. Cortines resigned to protest the mayor's plan to increase financial controls over the board, the Governor intervened to bring him back. Conversely, since the school board must approve the chancellor and can fire him at will, it can easily frustrate his initiatives. Cortines' predecessor, Joseph Fernandez, was ultimately fired for his efforts to institute a multicultural curriculum and condom distribution in City schools.

Such a pattern of struggle and hostility between school boards and superintendents is common in big cities. On average, big-city superintendents serve fewer than three years on the job; in 1990 the superintendencies of twenty of the twenty-five largest districts were vacant. Superintendents cite "interference and frustration" with the boards as one of the most important reasons for leaving. At the same time, and especially in large districts, the superintendent and the board are often controlled by the "permanent bureaucracy." For example, there are usually rigid formulae in place that allocate supplies, personnel, and other resources among schools. These rules further centralize the budgeting process outside the reach of either the board or the superintendent.

The relationship between boards and superintendents is generally much more cooperative in all but the largest districts. Most school-board members have no background in education and spend fewer than three years on the board, and so they tend to defer to and seek the guidance of the superintendent and his staff. Boards that do have a strong sense of what they want tend to hire or confirm only those superintendents who agree with them. In either case, there is seldom any real conflict. Most of a school board's time is consumed by the micromanagement of day-to-day school affairs. In West Virginia, for example, school boards must approve all field trips and spend only three percent of their time on policy-related matters. In California, boards must approve all expulsions. In Tucson, Arizona, the school board met 172 times in one year. Such day-to-day management is a far cry from the strategic, high-level board-of-directors model envisioned by the centralizers.

Schools That Run Themselves

Despite such instances of hyperactivity, the ability of school boards to make important policy decisions is steadily decreasing. In every state, central agencies have control over specific performance requirements for admission, certification, staffing, promotion, and graduation policies, and set the school day, the school term, and general policy. They also regulate nonpublic schools. Since most state constitutions specify that the state is responsible for maintaining the public schools, and school board members are agents of the state, the power they lend to local boards can be called in at any time, and has been.

Funding of schools has shifted from local districts to the states as well, prodded by the courts and state and federal title programs that mandate how significant sums of

Sources of Education Funds [4]			
	Local %	State %	Fed %
U.S. average	46.5	47.3	6.2
Hawaii	2.3	89.9	7.8
Nebraska	63.1	31.0	5.9
New Hampshire	89.4	7.8	2.8
New Mexico	15.1	72.7	12.2
Oregon	68.5	25.4	6.1
Washington	22.2	72.1	5.7

money must be spent. Nationwide, less than half of the funding for schools is raised locally, though there's wide variation.

During the 1980's, numerous state-level reforms forced changes in school financing and, coupled with federal and state education initiatives, took more control from local boards. As schools became a hot political issue, citizens elected governors and state legislators who ran on the promise of increased state-level control.

They delivered. Between 1980 and 1988, forty new state testing programs were put into effect. Between 1980 and 1986, more than one thousand separate pieces of state legislation regarding teacher pay and certification were introduced. These and other regulations all got states even more involved in specifying, monitoring, and certifying what goes on in schools.

As a result of this, school boards, once the voice of the community, today have little role in the conduct of the most important aspects of policy. The voters have already recognized this: at this point, only ten to fifteen percent of voters participate in school-board elections, and even fewer attend regular meetings. School-board elections are seldom issue-oriented, and few incumbents are ever turned out of office. For the most part, school boards are redundant, serving no useful policy or administrative function that could not just as easily be served by direct interactions among the state, parents, and the schools themselves.

The greater the number of school districts in a state, the greater is the cost of administrative overhead, since each district will generally have its own superintendent, its own business administrator, its own director of special education, and so on. New Jersey, for instance, has 611 school districts for 1.1 million students; Connecticut has a scant seventeen districts for 490,000 students. Some of New Jersey's fully staffed school districts don't even operate any schools, sending kids instead to neighboring districts. Why do New Jersey residents pay to support this? Perhaps because they fear integration.

Some localities are doing just that. Chicago, Rochester, and Miami, for instance, have done away with school boards. In these cities, parents, teachers, and citizens are elected to less powerful local community councils that choose principals and approve budgets. In Minnesota, schools can choose to affiliate with the state rather than with local districts. Massachusetts has initiated a bold plan known as "charter schools." Under this plan any group—parents, musicians, the Boston Museum of Science—can petition the state superintendent to allow them to open a school and receive public funding. If their proposal is accepted, they are free to teach whatever they want, however they want, and hire anyone they wish to teach and run the school. The teachers' union and the local boards, naturally, banded together to oppose the plan, which passed anyway with broad support.

The Feds

For nearly two hundred years the federal government played almost no significant role in education. The establishment and governance of schools predates the federal government, and running schools has always been regarded as one the powers specifically reserved by the states. Until after the Civil War, Congress repeatedly refused to maintain committees on education on the grounds that doing so would overstep federal authority.

Although a Department of Education was established in 1867, it was quickly demoted to the status of a bureau within the Department of the Interior where it languished unnoticed for nearly a hundred years. Even during the struggle surrounding the Supreme Court's 1954 landmark desegregation decision in *Brown v. Board of Education*, the Department of Education played only a minor role. Until the 1960s, the only significant federal education programs were those of the nineteenth century directed at Native Americans and newly freed slaves.

It took the Cold War and the War on Poverty to get the federal government directly involved with schools. In the shadow of *Sputnik*, a vexed and fretful nation embraced the 1958 National Defense Education Act as a means of strengthening math and science education in the high schools, which by this time were attended by eighty-five to ninety percent of children aged fourteen to seventeen. In 1965 the Elementary and Secondary Education Act, a centerpiece of the Great Society programs, made massive amounts of federal aid available to schools on the local level. Most of it went for programs for the disadvantaged like Head Start (Title I), as well as for

> *Prior to the 1960's, the federal policies that had the greatest impact on schools were not even directed at them. Transportation policy and road building, for example, made possible the consolidation of thousands of small, scattered rural districts. This diluted some of the local control, but at the same time permitted communities to pool their resources for programs that they would not have been able to afford on their own. In 1937, there were 119,000 separate school districts; in 1960, 40,000; and in 1990, 16,000. Around 50 percent of all districts still enroll fewer than 1,000 students.*

> *The 1867 law provided "That there shall be established at the City of Washington, a department of education, for the purpose of collecting such statistics and facts as shall show the condition and progress of education in the several States and Territories, and of diffusing such information respecting the organization and management of schools and school systems, and methods of teaching, as shall aid the people of the United States in the establishment and maintenance of efficient school systems, and otherwise promote the cause of education throughout the country."*

libraries, textbooks, and educational research laboratories (Titles II and III). During the 1970s, Federal involvement waxed and waned, with the largest increases going for drug education programs. Then came what has been called the "Reagan Reversion."

The Gipper

In 1983, the Carnegie Foundation report titled "A Nation at Risk" made education a hot issue, and focused attention on the connection between the quality of our educational system and the health of the economy. Although he had said little about education during his campaign and the early stages of his first term, President Reagan took up the fight, shifting the terms of the discussion about schools from "equity," which had been the thrust of federal education policy for the past twenty years, to "excellence." Not surprisingly, this fit well with his plans to cut aid to schools, since equity generally costs money (increased funding to poor school districts), and excellence does not (since it's mostly talk).

Soon Reagan was campaigning for drastically reduced federal spending on schools, as well as for changes in other school policy. He cut federal aid to public schools by twenty-five percent. He proposed legislation to put "reasonable limits" on the rights of handicapped kids to basic school services, and expressed his personal support for antibusing legislation while directing the Justice Department to withhold its assistance from those seeking to bring school desegregation suits. Finally, he endorsed tuition tax credits for private and parochial schools and proposed the abolition of the Department of Education. William Bennett (and his successor under George Bush, Lamar Alexander) positioned themselves as champions of excellence, opponents of an educational establishment that resisted such common-sense ideas as assessment and merit pay and cared only for the perpetuation of its own mediocrity.

Reagan's strategy was to head off opposition to what looked suspiciously like a retreat from public schooling. He asserted that it was precisely because education *was* so important that the federal government should play a smaller role. He used the populist language of local control to place responsibility with the states while at the same time reducing their ability to fund the excellence of which his administration spoke. Bennett energetically asserted that there was nothing wrong with American schools that couldn't be fixed with more homework for kids, more tests for teachers, and more authority for principals. In the meantime, though, the Department of Education lost one-third of its staff during the Reagan-Bush era, more than any other federal agency.

The Clinton administration has so far been relatively inactive in the area of education, although the Secretary of Education, Richard Riley, was one of the more successful "education governors" of the 1980s. It has supported and seen the passage of the Goals 2000 legislation begun by Bush and supported the reauthorization of the Elementary and Secondary Education Act through which most federal money finds its way to local schools. Many are expecting a big public push on education from the Administration during 1995.

National Goals

Federal policy not directly aimed at education, such as the promotion of a sophisticated National Information Infrastructure, is likely to once again have the greatest effect on schools. The connection of increasingly common school computer networks to the Internet is giving teachers and students access to a staggering array of resources they would never be able to acquire on their own. Many states are looking closely at how this new technology can be used to support school restructuring and teacher development. There are even those who believe that such learning technologies will cause schools to disappear altogether. Although such techno-utopian predictions are nearly always wrong, few doubt that the increasing use of networked microcomputers in schools can have a more profound effect on what schools do than have any technologies since the textbook and the blackboard.[3]

> *Every time a new technology appears, people predict it will revolutionize schools. Radio and TV were each going to make teachers expendable, and the airplane was going to change the study of geography and history (to study the Great Lakes, for example, you would just go there). We probably shouldn't sell off school real estate just yet.*

The mission of American schools has changed over the years—from moral compass to quasi-prison to factory training place to economic engine. Similarly, control over what goes on in classrooms has shifted significantly from the school building to local boards to the states. The national–standards movement and federally mandated programs shift it even further.

If we are to make schools more effective while making them more responsive, flexible, and diverse, we will need to revisit these issues, finding a system that can accommodate many differing goals, and mediate the debate between local and central control.

The Textbook That Nuked Korea

Who's in Charge Here?

Who do you think currently has the biggest say in your children's education? Is it the federal government? The state government? Teachers? The school board?

It may surprise you to learn that the answer is (to use a cliché) "none of the above." In fact, most curricular decisions are made by people whose names neither you, your kids, nor their teachers would ever recognize. They are the people who design, produce, and approve the textbooks with which students spend up to 90 percent of their instructional time and that have become as central to our notions of school as desks and blackboards.

Textbook publishing is an enormous industry that receives more than two billion taxpayer dollars every year. It has frequently been corrupt, and is always more concerned with what will sell than what is best for kids. As we'll show, the textbook publishing industry is one of the single most powerful forces in shaping the character and content of what your kids do in school. If they're not learning, or if they're not learning the right things, a great deal of the responsibility can be laid squarely at the feet of the textbook publishers.

One-stop Shopping

After teachers, textbooks are one of the oldest and most entrenched of school technologies, having existed in more or less the same form for almost 270 years. Noah Webster, the author of the eponymous dictionary, got his start in the business of standardizing American spelling with his "blue-backed speller" in 1783. In 210 years it has never been out of print. Probably the most popular textbooks ever, the McGuffey's Reader series, first published in 1856, sold more than 120 million copies by 1920.

Textbooks in general are so successful because they are ideally suited to the needs and purposes of mass schooling. They're standardized, portable, self-pacing, and relatively inexpensive. Out of an average school district expenditure of $4,000 per child in 1986, only $34 went to instructional materials. Textbooks collect in one convenient package all of the information a teacher is likely to use for a yearlong course, and they often come equipped with supplementary materials like handouts, homework sheets, exams, and floppy disks. They also cover everything that is likely to be taught for the standardized tests by which schools are evaluated.

For American teachers, who teach more classes per day than teachers in just about every other first-world country, textbooks save the time and effort that would be required to put together a course from original sources. Without textbooks, with their end-of-chapter review questions and prepackaged homework assignments, teachers would have to invest the time and energy to devise these assignments on their own, and time and energy are in notoriously short supply among people who juggle five classes of twenty–eight kids every day. Textbooks save school districts and administrators the burden of having to stock the wide inventory of books and supplies that would be required if instructors chose their own materials. If states pre-approve a list of textbooks from which districts, schools, or teachers then select, as many do, teachers and administrators are further relieved of the responsibility of making their own selections, thus sidestepping the possibility of parental dissatisfaction with the teachers' choice of curriculum.

In West Virginia in 1974, a Kanawha County textbook protest led to school boycotts, miners' strikes, school bombings, and police-escorted school buses being fired on with shotguns. The books were the subject of a lawsuit in which they were called "disrespectful of authority and religion, destructive of social and cultural values, obscene, pornographic, [and] unpatriotic." According to the American Library Association's Office of Intellectual Freedom, attempts to remove textbooks or other school materials account for the majority of censorship activity in the U.S.

Consequently, most teachers and administrators, as well as most parents, can no more easily imagine school without textbooks than life without schools themselves.

This reliance on textbooks has a price, however. In the process of organizing education around textbooks, we cede the role of curriculum design and implementation to large commercial publishing companies whose motivation is to produce the most widely acceptable product. In order to understand why this is so harmful to our kids' education, we need to look behind the scenes at how textbooks are produced and marketed.

Instructional materials are an important staple of the publishing industry. Elementary and high school sales account for more than 15 percent of all books sold in this country. Once a textbook has been accepted for use in a few large states, the publishers are guaranteed sales of several million books each year. The combination of the size of the market and the predictability of profits is one of the reasons why, during the last fifteen years, independent textbook publishers have been bought up and folded into much larger publishing (and nonpublishing) conglomerates. Eighty percent of the textbook market is now controlled by just seven publishers, with the Big Three—Macmillan, Harcourt Brace Jovanovich, and Simon & Schuster—controlling 45 percent among them.[1]

> *Harcourt Brace is an arm of Harcourt General which also owns General Cinema , one of the country's largest theater operators, which also owns the Neiman-Marcus and Bergdorf Goodman department stores (just to keep busy, General Cinema also underwrites accident, health, and life insurance policies.) Simon & Schuster—as well as Prentice Hall—is owned by the media conglomerate Viacom.*

The Bigger the Better?

Size is an advantage in the textbook business because a publisher can easily spend a million dollars to bring a new textbook or, more expensive and more profitable still, a new series of textbooks, to market. In order to be certain of making that money back, publishers need to land really big deals. Their chances of doing so are greatly aided by the fact that twenty-two states have centralized textbook adoption programs. Under such policies, a state-level committee or department chooses a handful of textbooks to make up an approved list. Every school in the state, if it wants state funding for its purchases, must choose books from that list. If a publisher can persuade an adoption committee to place its books on the adoption list, it can be assured of a predictable flow of profits for the life of that adoption cycle, usually from five to seven years.

Many states centralized textbook adoption around the turn of the century as a means of combating what were seen as abusive and corrupt practices by the "book trusts" of Northeastern publishers. Populist sentiment in the rural South and Southwest reacted especially strongly against allegations that shoddy materials were being pushed through with bribes and kickbacks to school super-intendents. It was also widely felt at the time that teachers and principals were too poorly trained to properly select classroom materials on their own. The centralization and formalization of textbook selection was thus a solution for ensuring that books would be acquired at the lowest cost, that the selection process would be carried out by "experts," and that students across the state would have equal access to the same high-quality materials.

Textbook vendors will do whatever they have to to get books adopted. They maintain large staffs of marketing and sales people whose job is to stay in touch with school systems across the country in order to anticipate and influence their needs. Large sums are spent to lobby state boards to choose one book over another or even to alter administrative procedures. At one point, the Merrill company (which was taken over by McGraw-Hill in 1990) spent $300,000 just to lobby the state of Texas to change its adoption schedule for math textbooks. Of course, Merrill's competitors turned around and spent even more money trying to counteract these effects.

Publishers naturally attempt to anticipate what selection committees will want to see in a textbook. The easiest way to do this is to give the boards more of what they've used in the past. This approach finds favor with many teachers because the books are familiar and don't require them to learn new skills or information. In order to clinch the deal, textbook publishers spend tens of thousands of dollars every year to entertain the teachers and administrators who serve on textbook committees. Selection committee members frequently receive free equipment, supplies, subscriptions, and other "contributions." Publishers, in fact, expect to spend much more money "promoting" textbooks than they do for trade books. It takes real money to play this game.

Pleasing All of the People

Textbook publishers naturally try to win places on the lists of as many states as possible. In practice, this means creating textbooks that are extremely broad in scope in order to sell into the differing curricula of many states and districts. Superficial responses to recent demands for a more inclusive attitude toward the accomplishments of women and minorities have exacerbated this problem: In order to grab the multicultural market, textbook writers have added mentions of dozens of new figures, rather than give in-depth treatment to just a few. This approach is rewarded by the practice of many state reviewers who prefer not to read the books carefully, but simply scan their tables of contents to see if the books conform to whatever criteria is under scrutiny.

Books like these are not written by authors but by <u>committees</u>, teams of junior staffers who may never meet one another and who generally lack real expertise in the subjects on which they write. It shows. In history books, for example, the need to include an over-large number of names and events causes them to lose all sense of narrative, of a story to be told. The very word "history" comes from the Latin for "a narrative of past events, an account, tale, or story." Real history books, in strong contrast to history textbooks, tell a strong and compelling story that helps the reader to make sense of the events described by placing them in a social, moral, and political context. Take a look at a modern history textbook and you're likely to find a disconnected catalog of places, names, and events.

If it's a textbook for the lower grades, you're in for an especially unpleasant reading experience because adoption committees typically require publishers to abide by what are perversely called "readability formulae." These regulations specify maximum allowable lengths for the words and sentences that make up books at each grade level. They turn what ought to be a pleasurable and stimulating encounter with language and ideas into an ordeal of forced semiliteracy. For some reason, it never seems to occur to anyone that one reason kids don't read their textbooks is because they aren't worth reading, or that the reason they write so poorly is that their textbooks present them with such bad models.

> *Richard Feynman, the Nobel Prize–winning physicist, was once asked to serve on a California textbook review committee. At one point in the process he was given a handsomely bound book that contained nothing but blank pages, presumably the result of one of the printing errors that are not uncommon when books are produced in limited runs, as they are when sample copies are run off. Feynman naturally made no comment on the book. His fellow panelists, he discovered the next day, were less reticent. They had given the blank book high marks and recommended that it be approved for adoption. It is well established within the textbook industry that money spent on sizzle—illustrations, four-color photographs, expensive binding—yields a better return than money spent developing high-quality content.*

Nuking Korea

To the publishers, following these state-imposed guidelines is just good business. But bad business is what can happen when such assembly-line approaches to authorship and oversight are coupled with an indifference to content. In 1992, independent reviewers in Texas found more than 5,200 factual errors in history textbooks submitted to the state by major publishers. Some were minor, but the list included gaffes like claims that the U.S. used nuclear weapons to end the Korean War; that we sent troops to invade Cuba during the Bay of Pigs; and that *Sputnik* was a Soviet missile carrying a nuclear warhead.

These mistakes were discovered only *after* the textbooks had been examined and approved for a $20 million purchase by both the state textbook review committee and the staff of the Texas Education Agency. The publishers paid fines of hundreds of thousands of dollars in order to get corrected versions of the books accepted, and were forced into embarrassing public admissions that the errors were due to poor fact-checking, bad manuscripts, and their own inability to meet deadlines. By the time Texas discovered the errors, the books were already in use in school systems around the country.

> For a particularly enjoyable and coherent analysis of the twelve bestselling American History textbooks, read "Lies My Teacher Told Me" by Prof. James Loewen of the University of Vermont.

Workmanship this shoddy is unusual, although the level of the publishers' contempt for their market unfortunately is not. More unsettling still, is a practice that textbook publishers follow all too frequently, one that ends up affecting the quality, honesty, and accuracy of what goes on in classrooms from coast to coast. We're speaking of the practice, freely admitted to by textbook company representatives, of modifying the content and focus of their curricula to suit the religious and political views of the centralized-adoption states.

The Rules of Adoption

Most states don't have centralized textbook adoption policies. Since buying decisions are made on a local level, none of them constitutes an important unified market for the publishers to woo. Even the largest nonadoption states like New York or Illinois do not have much influence over what publishers include or leave out of textbooks, because publishers know that each school or district is free to use whatever books they like. On the other hand, the minority of states that do have adoption policies, nearly all of them southern or western states, exercise tremendous influence over the content of the textbooks used not only in their schools but by the entire country.

According to a survey released by the American Association of Publishers in 1981, "textbook publishers can rarely afford to turn away sales in a major adoption state. Nor can they, in most cases, afford the luxury of maintaining two separate editions. Thus an edition prepared for Texas or California . . . often becomes the sole edition available nationwide."

The sheer size of its school system combined with its fully centralized adoption procedures makes Texas the 900-pound gorilla of the textbook market. In 1982 alone, sales of textbooks proposed for statewide adoption in Texas exceeded $60 million. What Texas wants, Texas gets.

Each year the Texas State Board of Education issues the Texas Textbook Proclamation, which lays out the official guidelines for textbook content and structure. According to administrative procedure any citizen may challenge any textbook that is put up for consideration. This has frequently resulted in the textbooks of the entire country being held hostage to the values of Texas' religious extremists. According to a 1983 report by the *People For The American Way* Texas Textbook Project:

> *California is the largest overall market for textbooks in the country, with over 5 million K–12 students (about 50 percent more than Texas). It has somewhat less influence on publishers, however, because it permits schools to choose from a wider variety of books on the K-8 level and allows districts to choose whatever books they like on the high school level.*

Publishers readily admit that textbook changes are made if necessary to get their books on the Texas-approved lists. Changes made to meet Texas demands often become changes in textbooks used throughout the country. In 1981, hoping to make the American Heritage Dictionary acceptable for Texas classrooms, Houghton Mifflin publishing representatives offered to delete "offensive words" from the latest edition. In 1980, to placate Texas critics, publishers precensored Shirley Jackson's classic 1949 short story "The Lottery" from the national editions of four literature anthologies.

Tom Giblin, assistant superintendent of the Widefield school district in Colorado Springs, told a national television audience "a decision in Texas really does make a textbook. If there's an exclusion of something that Texas asked the publisher to do, we suffer that exclusion also in Colorado."

William Wood, of the Follett Publishing Company Juvenile Division told the *Dallas Times-Herald* "If we couldn't sell a book [in Texas] without creationism in it, I imagine you'd see it in there." Felix Laiche of Doubleday's textbook division said on PBS "If [the Texas Education Agency] backs us up against the wall and says, 'You either take it out or you won't sell the book in Texas,' then we'll take it out."

In the words of a major publishing representative, "We'll give them whatever they want; we don't care, if they just tell us what they want."

One of the things that religious extremists wanted—and got—in 1982 was the elimination of questions that lead to classroom discussions, questions like "what do you think of . . . ?" or "how would you react to . . . ?" Norma Gabler, a leader of the censorship movement, called such questions examples of "secular humanism." "Leaving students to make up their own minds about things just isn't fair to our children," she has said. "A concept will never do anyone as much good as a fact."

The fortunes of cultural extremists tend to wax and wane, and those of the Gablers have declined in recent years. Since 1990, Texas science and history books have even been allowed to teach the theory of evolution. Nevertheless, the potential for corruption in the centralized textbook adoption process by the strange-bedfellows collusion of censors and publishers is always present.

Special Interests

Sometimes the influence of special interest groups is subtle, as when Oregon decided to rewrite its social-studies textbooks in 1985 and 1987. Funding for the project was provided by the agricultural and timber industries, prompting a suit by those who felt that the textbooks reflected an excessively one-sided pro-industry bias in matters relating to environmental management. Sometimes that influence is overt, as with the pressures on New York school superintendent Joseph Fernandez over the multicultural curriculum which eventually led to his removal.

Despite their significance to their local constituencies, neither the Oregon nor the New York conflicts had much impact on other school systems, on the education of other people's children. Through the coincidence of public and private market forces, however, the process of centralized textbook adoption allows a board in Texas or California or Georgia to exercise "local control" over what teachers in New Jersey, Michigan, or Washington can use in their classrooms. It doesn't matter how good local adoption policies are in decentralized states, how aggressive and participatory the process is in seeking out the very best textbooks, because publishers don't write for that market. They write for Texas.

What's Wrong With This Picture?

Given the tremendous amounts of time that students spend with textbooks, the degree to which textbooks displace teachers, and their centrality to the experience of school, one would imagine that thinking about textbooks would be an integral part of any school reform plan.[2] Yet this is rarely the case. In fact, too many reform proposals contain the same kind of thinking about teaching, learning, and the administration of schools that contributed to the shortcomings of the present system.

Many plans for school reform proceed from the conviction that there is too much variation and not enough "expert" input or control. They seek to further centralize such decisions as who can be certified to teach, what their course of preparation must be, and how schools must be organized. As we'll see later, conventional national curriculum and national testing proposals are the epitome of this way of looking at school improvement, and uniform textbook adoption is part and parcel to it as well.

The roots of this movement, and of the standardization of public schooling in general, can be traced to the introduction of the "Carnegie unit" in 1909. Intended in part to ensure that schools provide a minimum quantity of instruction to all students, the Carnegie unit specified that high school courses would consist of 120 hours spread over thirty-six weeks, with classes meeting four or five days a week for about fifty minutes each. It is still used in every state to specify what constitutes an approved plan of study.

While the Carnegie unit did transform the high school diploma into a reliable indicator of how many hours a student had spent sitting in a classroom, it also removed from schools and school districts the ability to arrange for themselves the structures of education that suited their students best.

Textbooks are the logical tool of a curriculum organized into Carnegie units. Subject-specific, they divide fields of inquiry into sections that are easily covered in a single class period. Review questions at the end of each section reinforce the impression of self-contained chunks of information. Rather than the textbook serving as a resource for teachers, teachers become resources for the textbook, relieved of the authority and the responsibility to gather and organize subject matter into a form that is both stimulating and effective.

The Carnegie unit was the outgrowth of the work of a panel known as the Committee of Ten, which consisted of five college presidents, two headmasters, one professor, and one high school administrator (but no high school teachers). It was appointed by the NEA in 1892 to settle arguments between educational "modernists" and "traditionalists" over what schooling should consist of. The panel came down squarely on the side of the traditionalists, believing that only the classical organization of subject matter as practiced in European universities was fit to discipline young minds. Because of its stature, the Committee of Ten was able to persuade universities to make the completion of at least fourteen Carnegie units a prerequisite for college entrance, thus severely limiting the number and types of courses that students could take in high school and, for the first time, making a high school diploma a prerequisite for entrance to college.

Why Aren't Textbooks Better?

Even though teachers' unions often negotiate in their contracts for participation in textbook review processes, their participation has made little difference. Under their current forms of organization, schools and school workers have little to gain and much to lose from selecting innovative or even distinctive materials. When surveyed on what they value in textbooks, teachers expressed preferences for products that are easy to use, include a teacher's manual and other supplementary materials, and require little preparation. Studies of teacher attitudes towards new forms of instructional materials have typically shown responses ranging from indifference to anxiety.

Because we don't train or trust teachers to select good textbooks and curricula, we set up adoption committees and school boards to do it for them. These committees are generally held accountable only when the content of a book offends someone's sensibilities, but we routinely blame teachers and administrators for the failure of a curriculum. When teachers are unable to motivate their students with lousy textbooks, we never hold the people who wrote and chose the books responsible. Instead we blame the victims—teachers and students—who suffer from those bad decisions.

The Cure

We're not going to get better textbooks by passing new state mandates requiring them—that's what got us into this mess in the first place. And things won't change by themselves; publishers, teachers, school boards,

In chapter nine, we discuss changes in teacher training that would produce the skills to make these decisions competently.

and state agencies each have a vested interest in the continuation of this system. The solution must be structural. We need to to give teachers— the ultimate consumers of the product—a great deal more freedom to choose what best suits their needs.

Under the plan we'll set forth, schools and teachers would be accountable for their students' results and therefore would be given more latitude to choose the curricula they would teach and the tools they would use to help them. Ultimately, textbooks would compete in a market that looks much more like the marketplace described in, well, textbooks—the customers (teachers) will choose products (textbooks) on the basis of good information (correlations of textbook use against scores on national tests tied to each curriculum).

After all of this, you might be a bit skeptical that our proposal will create a new generation of competent textbooks. Before we demonstrate it, though, we need to discuss the link between testing and curricula.

The Übercurriculum

Anarchy

If you're a parent, sending your children to school can be like watching them being carried off and locked in the trunk of a car. During the school year, parents get occasional clues about their kids' whereabouts. At the end of the year, they're dropped off back at home.

Where were they? What were they supposed to have learned? Unless you look over their homework every day, you'll have no idea. Helping them with that homework, though, means guessing what the teacher is trying to convey, trying to grasp the direction from the assignments. And even if you figure out where the class has *been*, it's nearly impossible to discern where it's going.

At the end of the year, you can't judge whether your kids have learned anything. The final exam was written by the teacher—it provides some clue as to the content covered in the course. But how was it graded? Does a grade of 85 mean your daughter has learned a reasonable amount about the Industrial Revolution, that her writing style is good (or bad, perhaps—with grade inflation, an 85 at some schools is well below average), or that she has learned to think critically? Each school district in the country has a different set of standards, and every teacher has his or her own twist on those. This scenario makes it difficult to fairly hold teachers accountable, or to systematically supplement the teaching that takes place in the classroom.

Students and teachers can't transfer easily, since every school works on its own schedule, and every school means different things by "Algebra I" or "World History." Because most students switch schools at some point, almost everyone misses certain subjects and repeats others. With no common curriculum, textbooks have to include everything that any teacher anywhere might think is important, which helps makes textbooks fat and unfocused.

In a responsive, well–functioning system, you could find out what your children were learning and how well they were learning it. You would know how well their teachers taught one subject or another, and how their schools compared to others. It would mean that we would stop throwing away the lode of useful information generated *every day* in classrooms around the country, and mine it instead for clues as to what works best for all sorts of teachers and students.

If medical research worked like our schools, each doctor would figure out his or her own favorite cure for a disease, using no scientific data to justify that choice, and no follow up to see if the cure was effective. If your company ran like this, a supervisor would give each employee a desk and a phone, and look in on them from time to time to make sure they weren't using drugs or wasting too many paper clips.

Where America Learns

Variability is not the same as real variety. It's not the case that different schools are going off in all sorts of meaningfully different directions, exploring new approaches to the old problem of engaging kids in learning. There would great virtue in such variety, but that's not what we have now. Instead, we have schools trying to do very much the same things from school to school, from teacher to teacher, from year to year, but failing to do it consistently. This lack of consistency and accountability produces a lack of responsiveness, since there is nothing concrete for schools to respond to. This lack of responsiveness, this insulation of schools from the needs of their communities, only aggravates the mistrust that many people feel toward their schools.

We're not saying every school should be the same. But, as we'll discuss, to the degree that schools are trying to do the same thing, there are advantages to doing it consistently.

This sentiment prevails even in well-financed, well-equipped districts. The common impression is that large schools have become academic shopping malls, where students choose from a menu of trendy and insubstantial offerings. Schedules are crowded with nonacademic electives at the expense of the basics. As a result, even kids who put in their seat time for four years are ill-equipped for college or the job market. Many feel that this situation has only gotten worse in recent years with the advent of multicultural and social-values curricula that further detract from the time and focus devoted to the three R's.

Reactions like this have been present to a greater or lesser degree for twenty-five years, since the curricular reforms of the late sixties and early seventies. At that time, students, parents, and many teachers demanded a school curriculum that was "relevant" to their cultures and the times in which they lived. Big city schools in particular saw the rise of ethnic-studies programs, ecological studies, increased attention to the arts, and a shift in decision making over school hiring and course content from a previously centralized state or city authority to newly formed community boards. These changes were widely interpreted by those who favored the established ways of running schools as a "decline of academic standards," and word began to spread that students were leaving high school less and less qualified to perform even rudimentary tasks.

It's Black and White

To some extent, the perception of educational decline provided cover for the latest skirmish in the battles that began in the nineteenth century over the control of schools. As before, the combatants divided neatly along social and ethnic lines. Today, as twenty years ago and as one hundred years before that, the groups striving to gain or to hold on to control of school systems include people who feel that their cultures, their values, and their histories have been excluded from the image of American life that schools present to students. This is not to say that there is no substance to the claim that standards have changed, or that schools are doing a different job—and doing it differently—than they did thirty years ago. It does serve as a reminder that whether a change is an "empowerment" or a "decline in academic standards" often depends on what side you're on, and whether it is your ox that is being gored.

If we change the phrase "declining academic standards" to something like "reduced importance of academic achievement as a value for schools," we are looking at the issue from a different point of view. School reformers in the sixties and seventies were less concerned with making students into better scholars or employees than they were with explicitly addressing and redressing the ways in which schools had been organized and the relationship of schools to society at large. While the debate today centers

> *The everyday sense of "standards" has its roots in the factory floor and the churchyard, in our modern means of material improvement and our model means of moral improvement. That is why talk of standards for schools often has the scolding tone common to talk about standards of ethical behavior, and the practical, down-to-earth tone heard in talk about standards for, say, copper wire or computer networks.*

on why schools are performing their tasks poorly, reform efforts of the sixties and seventies questioned the very desirability of the tasks that schools were seen to perform, tasks like tracking, regimenting, and reproducing an inequitable society.

Under the scrutiny of widespread social criticism during the 1960s and 1970s, the tools and values upon which schools had traditionally relied—testing, standardization, exhortation, and discipline—lost credibility, but few effective replacements were consistently or reliably deployed to replace them. At the same time, school- reform discussions became politically polarized and loaded with code words. Asserting the importance of traditional academic standards and values was identified with a reactionary political agenda, while political progressives were stereotyped as favoring a mushy-headed disregard for measurable achievement.

Global Competition

In the sixties, America was still the preeminent global power in every respect. Although we had numerous enemies, we had no real competitors, and no threat to a seemingly infinite economic expansion that had seen the standard of living for blue– and white–collar workers alike rise to a level that was the envy of the world. The issues at stake in school reform at that time were about self-expression and fairness, not economic survival. School structure and content mattered so much precisely because schools were seen to be effective. They were assumed to have a real impact on the kids who went through them, and so their structure and content were of the utmost importance. People were concerned about *what* kids learned, not *whether* they did, and since the middle class had generally been in firm control of curriculum, school reform was not an issue that concerned them much except as something to oppose.

This is no longer the case. As the middle class has seen its situation erode over the past two decades, a kind of panic has set in. High school and even college diplomas no longer guarantee a good job. As more and more people move through the educational system without finding a decent job waiting at the other end, as America's international preeminence is challenged and its standard of living overtaken by that of several other countries, dissatisfaction is coming from all sides, from all classes.

Society's requirement of mandatory schooling for teenagers represents, after all, a bargain with them and their families: They agree to forego present earnings in return for the greater earning power enabled by a functional education. In the short run, society gets teenagers off the streets and out of Satan's clutches. In the long run, it is also supposed to be provided with citizens who are both productive workers and able to fulfill the requirements of democratic participation. This bargain is subscribed to by all families with children in schools, regardless of their class origins. As the nation endures a fundamental and painful economic restructuring, preparation for a changing society takes on even greater importance, both real and symbolic.

In times of crisis or perceived inadequacy, we tend to look to our schools for both scapegoats and solutions. Vocational education was established because of worries at the beginning of this century that America was becoming unable to compete industrially against Europe. The launching of *Sputnik* by the Soviets in 1957 intensified fears that we were falling behind technologically, and led to a tremendous commitment—at least rhetorically—to build up the math and science preparation of American teenagers. Now we're said to face a different sort of threat, not from militarized communism but from allies, the beneficiaries of our post-war generosity, who seek to dominate us economically. As before, a common response is to look toward schools and demand that they cut out the nonsense and prepare kids to reclaim our rightful place at the top of the heap. Once again, the rubric is competitiveness. If schools were doing their job properly, the reasoning goes (just as it went in 1910 and 1960), we would have better workers whose output would enable us to regain our global preeminence.

> *There is something a little absurd about holding today's schools responsible for systemic national and global shifts. After all, important decisions in our society are generally made by people in (at least) their forties. Thus, if we're going to attribute national competitiveness to the kinds of education people get in high school, then it is the education these middle-aged men received thirty years ago, the kind we are often told we should return to, that is responsible for the various messes in which we find ourselves. Similarly, changing what high schools do to kids will not have any conceivable effect on our corporate or political systems for at least another twenty years, when today's high-school kids begin to assume positions of authority.*

Goals 2000

In 1989, a panel of governors, formulating what would be called the America 2000 recommendations, declared that within ten years American students should, among other things, "lead the world in math and science" and "possess the skills necessary to compete in a global economy."

This was to be achieved through the establishment of curriculum standards and national achievement tests. The recommendations were promptly endorsed by George Bush and his Secretary of Education, Lamar Alexander. Congress concurred and established the National Council on Educational Standards and Testing to develop a series of tests that could be used to assess the performance of students across the country, as well as a series of targets called Goals 2000.

Some of the appeal of this get-down-to-business, back-to-basics approach is precisely the ways in which it differs from old experiments like new math and alternative schools. Curriculum standards and national testing are offered as the rigorous broom that will sweep away the muddle-headed muck and restore schools to their former glory. Even the American Federation of Teachers, long considered more radical and socially conscious than its rival, the NEA, announced its support for a national curriculum.

Such proposals for standardization—whether of assessment or curricula—have simplicity and directness as their main virtues. What they want to teach and test is laid out in detail, as are the methods and criteria for assessment. Important decisions about the curriculum are made by panels of experts, while the schools' jobs are simply to ensure that kids are spending enough seat time in the designated subject areas, doing plenty of appropriate homework, and taking tests on a regular basis. Unlike many other proposals for rejuvenating schools, this one seems simple, even-handed, and inexpensive. For most people over forty, this vision of schools is familiar and comfortable. It reminds them, they think, of what school was like for them.

Proposals for a single national curriculum, like all ideas for education reform that capture some part of the public imagination, contain elements that speak to a genuine sense of frustration with the existing state of schooling. The rationalizing of a curriculum, the design of relevant assessment, and the institution of accountability that are central to national curriculum thinking have real appeal and real value. Having one curriculum creates a straightforward system of accountability for performance. Everyone is teaching the same thing at the same time, so everyone can be judged by the same tests, which are specifically geared to that curriculum. Parents know exactly what their children are supposed to be learning, and whether they are in fact learning it. Since all schools are teaching the same thing and using the same tests to assess it, the better schools and teachers are easy to find.

Who Shall Set the Standards?

Behind a national curriculum is an attempt to institute accountability and create a diagnostic tool for identifying poorly performing students, teachers, and schools. Such a system could establish benchmarks for performance, and allow us to compare the performance of kids from different schools or different states. National tests could, theoretically, be carefully calibrated and kept free of overt bias, and could help us learn what we do well and poorly.

Unfortunately, benchmarks, especially national ones, are tricky things. Theodore Sizer, for many years a leader in school reform, has asked "Who shall set the standards? And by what right?" For better or for worse, our tradition of education is built on the rights of communities to have a say in what their children will study and how they will be judged. A national curriculum, though it would tend to increase accountability, would drastically decrease the responsiveness of schools to community needs and wishes. Most Americans are unlikely to be satisfied with such a trade–off.

Nor are performance comparisons by themselves even very useful in education. For instance, national testing plans seldom suggest what, if anything, should first be done for students who aren't being educated now so that they're not penalized later by a test for which they're not prepared. When educational conditions are as wildly unequal as they are in our country, a plan which treats all students "equally" is in practice as deeply unfair as expecting wheelchair athletes to post the same qualifying times as Olympic medalists. Most national-standards plans also have little to say about what to do when underachievers are identified. It is one thing to diagnose those students, teachers, or schools who need extra help and then provide it to them, and quite another to use their scores as a means of denying them opportunities for improvement so that they can advance.

During the eighties, for example, many states introduced _gate-tests_, competency tests given every few grades to make sure the students are ready for promotion. Although these tests seem reasonable in principle, they haven't worked out that way in practice. Most states using competency tests are southern. Most of the failing students are black.[1] Almost no state allocates a significant amount of money to help weaker students catch up, and so the gate-testing ends up constituting a kind of tracking even within one-track systems. Students who are left back often drop out rather than face their former classmates at school every day. Finally, there has been little improvement in student outcomes in schools using these tests.

Of course, we already have some experience with national tests in the form of college admissions exams like the SAT and ACT, SAT II Subject Tests (formerly the Achievements), and Advanced Placement Tests, and federally sponsored tests like the National Assessment of Educational Performance (NAEP). The differences among these tests is illustrative of the problems we would face in designing a palatable exam to support a national curriculum.

There are basically two types of exams in the world: *high-stakes*, where the outcome has real consequences for those it measures; and *low-stakes*, where it doesn't. The NAEP exams are good examples of low-stakes tests. Since the results make no difference to students, many kids don't take them seriously (why should they?), and individual performance varies wildly. The overall data may be of some use in judging broad populations, but it can do almost nothing to help evaluate specific teaching strategies or individual student performance.

> Even if you don't think you've heard of NAEP, you have. Every six months or so, front-page articles appear with its latest, inevitably depressing, findings. Perhaps for the reasons mentioned here, students taking NAEP can't find their shorts, much less Miami.

In a broad sense, low-stakes tests may manage to measure—without wasting too much time and energy—a subset of what is taught in school. Absent a national curriculum, however, there just aren't that many things that every teacher in every school is teaching at exactly the same time. Consequently these tests give only the slightest clue as to the quality of instruction in a classroom.

High Stakes

College admissions tests are good examples of high-stakes tests because they're taken by a self-selecting population of students to whom the results matter a lot. The reputation of many high schools, in turn, depends on how their graduates fare in the college admissions game, so the results matter to them as well. In addition, politicians and the press often—and quite wrongly—use a state's average SAT scores as an indicator of educational quality.

> The SAT claims to be a test of reasoning skills, not learned knowledge. Until recently, the "A" in SAT stood for Aptitude, or natural ability; now it stands for Assessment, making this the Scholastic Assessment Test, the only redundantly named English exam in the country.

As a result, a great deal of attention is paid to the SAT, far too much for a test that *by design* does not attempt to test what kids have learned in high school.

Our experience at The Princeton Review is instructive here. When we started the company in 1981, test coaches tried to portray what they were doing as educational. Not only would they raise scores, but they would make your child smarter and better educated. The Princeton Review put things in simpler terms—we will help raise your scores, period. Very little in our ads about math or English. Nothing about making you better read or better prepared for college. "When they put Shakespeare on the SAT, we'll teach Shakespeare." Focused on the test itself, we did a very good job preparing students. Within seven years, we were the largest SAT course in the country, and our competition either disappeared or dropped anything extraneous (i.e., not on the test) from their courses. Now, nearly every student taking the SAT prepares for it in one way or another.

This makes sense. The SAT is critically important to students, teachers, and schools. College admission rides on SAT scores, as do most merit-based scholarships. Real estate agents compare test scores of school districts, newspapers compare college football programs by the test scores of their players. One of the consequences of our hodgepodge of educational assessment is that people will look for measures of academic excellence wherever they can find them, even in the wrong places.

While this emphasis on the SAT has been good for test preparation companies, it has arguably been less so for the quality of education in general. As the success of TPR called attention to the fact that it was indeed possible to raise SAT scores significantly, it also placed pressure on schools and teachers to devote less class time teaching kids English and math and more time prepping them for the SAT. Over the past decade, junior year in many schools has come to seem like one long SAT prep course. In some cases, it literally is. A few years ago, South Carolina decided it would no longer have the worst test scores of any state. It replaced junior-year English with SAT prep, raised its average scores considerably, and climbed to number 49. As if on cue, the press then heralded South Carolina as an educational success story. (Unfortunately, it's now back to number 50, trailing Georgia by six points.)

A bizarre cycle occurs when schools are measured by test scores. Since no one mandates what all schools teach, we can only measure what is common to all of them, a "lowest common denominator". This not only forces every school to teach certain material, it rewards those who teach it to the exclusion of anything else, because they can be more focused than schools that teach other material as well. Thus, half-hearted standards actually *lower* the bar. Just as many students will not study material that won't be covered on the test, most schools will do the same thing. As you limit the range of material covered on an important test, you ultimately limit the schools themselves. Professor James Popham of UCLA notes that if "measurement driven instructional programs install low-level and trivial assessment targets for their high stakes tests, then it is patently clear that educators will devote too much time to the pursuit of such puerile outcomes."

Some admissions counselors argue that the SAT is not as important as most students believe. Grades, they say, count more than test scores, and they're right. But if the SAT is only 75 percent as important as grades, this one three-hour test is as important as *three years* of high school. This is too high a stake for any test that measures so little so poorly.

A Silver Lining?

One happy insight that can be gained by looking at the SAT world is that people are willing to spend a fair amount of money for education if they have some confidence that it's working. At the same time that every school in the country is gasping for the money to continue its programs and hold class sizes down, the U.S. is spending well over $100 million a year preparing for this one test.

Of course, the rich are spending more than the poor. Most kids who prep are using fifteen-dollar books or forty-dollar software. Some are involved in inexpensive or subsidized courses that meet a few times, while others are spending over $600 for intensive courses like ours. And a few are spending up to $3,000 working with tutors who left law practices because they didn't pay enough.

The Princeton Review has been successful because we're accountable. We're up-front about what we promise and what we expect of our students in turn. Our success can be measured as easily as comparing before–and–after SAT scores. We hold our teachers responsible not only for students' scores but for their enjoyment of the course. Our course directors in turn are liable not only for their teachers' performance but for the satisfaction of the parents who have trusted us to do a job. Crucially, however, this accountability exists *not* because we're a private company or because of market pressure; it is the flip side of our ability to work toward our goals in the ways we think best.

If we can create an educational system that's accountable and responsive enough, it's possible that people—parents and legislators—will be willing to give schools the discretion to teach as they think best. They may even be willing to spend more on education. Then again, it's possible they won't have to.

The English Test

The most sweeping institution of national testing accompanied the over-haul of Britain's school system, begun in 1988 by Conservative prime min-ister Margaret Thatcher. Starting with English and math, and then spreading to science, religion, and history, the British national curriculum set yearly tests in each subject.

It has not worked out well. Parents and teachers who were initially enthusiastic about the national-curriculum reforms have reacted strongly against what they feel has proven to be a narrow, doctrinaire approach to education.[2] Former supporters have discovered that when you institute a standardized test that has real consequences, a component essential to national-curriculum plans, teachers teach specifically to that test and little else. Students spend their time on the rote assimilation of facts and figures rather than on developing the kinds of higher-order thinking skills that are claimed to be important in the emerging Information Age. Teachers and principals have less leeway to or-ganize and teach what and how they want, which is, of course, exactly what a national curriculum intends. Even *The Economist* has concluded that "the government has made a hash of things."

> According to studies, about a sixth of educators believe it's appropriate to prepare students for a test by showing them the test itself, and the majority believe it's appropriate to teach only question formats that will appear on the test itself.[3]

The fundamental problem with high-stakes testing is that it works. It works so well, in fact, that those whom it affects—teachers, students, school administrators—tend to focus on The Test to the exclusion of much else.

In the British example, kids did assimilate the facts that the test writ-ers required them to know but at the expense of spontaneity, discovery, and—according to reports—learning how to think for themselves. The case of the SAT is even worse, as the course of study that best prepares students for it—and we should know—has little academic value.

Assessment tests only make sense when they are bound to a specific course of study. If that curriculum is a good one, and if the test reflects the knowledge and skills that curriculum attempts to instill, then teaching to that test would not be a bad thing at all. The best test, of course, is one in which learning something worthwhile is itself the best preparation. Such tests do exist.

For example, The College Board's AP (Advanced Placement) tests measure how well a student has done in a very challenging high-school course. Based on these tests, high-school students can earn college credits in twelve subjects. The AP tests have spawned an entire tier of high-school courses. These are pretty tough courses, generally the most rigorous a school offers. Unlike tests that try to measure a basic competency, and hence encourage a teacher to teach less, a good curriculum-bound test presents a challenge to a teacher: how to teach this curriculum as efficiently and effectively as possible.

The APs, of course, aren't appropriate for every student, every subject, or every school. First of all, they're extremely tough, intended only for high-level students. Second, their content and format are not determined by the teacher or the school and so require an acceptance of someone else's idea of what the best course of study is. If every history teacher were required to teach that history covered by the History AP, we would lose a lot of great history teachers.

Inputs versus Outputs

The standards that state boards have been setting for schools for nearly a century—classroom hours per day, the number of courses required for graduation, or mandated teacher-preparation programs—are basically input standards. Input standards dictate precisely how the job must be done, but don't hold you responsible for how the work turns out. Output standards, by contrast, say, "This is the result we want. You figure out how to get there."

In the engineering world, the analogs of these are design and performance specifications. If you wanted a bridge built to design specifications, you would put out a bid that said, "The bridge must have clear span of 3,500 feet, have two blue towers, be composed of 42,000 tons of steel, and possess four main cables three feet in diameter with 243,000 strands of steel each." Performance specification for such a bridge might read, "The bridge must cross the Hudson River, and be capable of carrying 100 cars and 65 trucks each minute, at an average speed of 45 miles per hour." Most real-world systems have moved away from design specifications. Instead, they rely on performance specifications because these tend to stimulate designers and contractors to come up with innovative solutions that get the job done better, more easily, or less expensively.

People are generally either creative, motivated by profit, or both, and performance specifications tap those incentives to best effect. If a bridge that fulfills design specification collapses, there's no way you can blame the builders. Performance specifications, on the other hand, make the designers and engineers responsible for what they produce. Similarly, if schools have no choice in what they teach, how they teach it, what materials they use, or who does the teaching, it is simply unreasonable to hold them responsible for the quality of the students they produce.

That's a basic problem with most national-testing plans. They'll be used to evaluate schools that have no say in developing or choosing the tests and no real freedom to change what they do in order to perform better. In the absence of a national curriculum, such tests won't even be closely linked to what schools are teaching. Good curriculum–bound tests *can* be a vantage point from which to evaluate teaching and learning. Once in place, such tests should eventually give people enough confidence in their ability to judge school performance that input standards become unnecessary. Schools would then be free to pursue the goals set for them in the ways they think best.

That's not the system we have now, though. While a single national curriculum would introduce more accountability than currently exists, we would still need to decide whether the costs of such a program—decreased teacher autonomy, student choice, and systemic responsiveness—are worth the gains in accountability.

The Ideology of Standardization

Standardized tests and national curricula, like most designs for grand educational reform, are the products of a distinct way of viewing the world. Uniformity, assessment, and centralized control are the hallmarks of these plans, and they tend to be promoted more heavily by conservatives than by liberals or moderates. There is some irony here, since conservatives are in most other matters said to be partial to a diminished role for central authority, while liberals allegedly support an increased federal presence in people's lives. While it is too simple to think that a political label can predict someone's position on an issue like this, national curriculum and back-to-basics proposals did receive their strongest federal advocacy during the tenures of Ronald Reagan and George Bush.

The linking of school reform with a political agenda, especially one prone to moralizing about "declining standards," makes many people wary. They worry that a national curriculum (and the tests used to assess it) would carve in stone the local, time- and culture-bound circumstances of its developers. This, in turn, would reduce both community control and the flexibility to adopt new ways of thinking about schools.

Dead White Men

While England's experience serves as an example of the dangers a national curriculum and test might pose, it's unlikely that America would ever get that far with a similar plan. A national curriculum presupposes a consensus on what should be taught that we would likely find very difficult to achieve. About the same time that we began discussing national standards for our high schools, a fierce and bitter debate began at universities over what college students should be taught. On one side are the proponents of multiculturalism, who say that the homogenizing cultural hegemony exerted by the works of "dead white men" serves to perpetuate a narrow, biased way of imagining the world. This self-serving provincialism, they argue, deprives us of the rich diversity of contributions made (and being made) by the majority of people in the world who are neither dead, nor white, nor men.

On the other side are those who say that it behooves students to understand American, and hence Western, culture and history before embracing those of others. It seems ludicrous to remove Shakespeare, Milton, and Whitman from the curriculum in order to replace them with African, Asian, and Native American poets. Multiculturalism, they argue, is a quota system—discrimination in reverse—in which a place in the curriculum is secured not by merit but by passing an ethnicity- or gender-based litmus test. If a curriculum is going to mandate specific distribution requirements, why favor African history over American history? Why go out of your way to eliminate Plato and Aristotle? Why stress the differences between Americans rather than the heritage we hold in common?

Each side in this war portrays itself as the underdog, victim of suppression and persecution by the mindless self-interested orthodoxy of powerful opponents. "Communist" and "fascist" are no longer much hurled as epithets at universities these days: Now "politically correct" and "cultural imperialist" are the terms of choice to really slander those with whom you disagree.

Mandatory Dead White Men

As acrimonious as this debate has become, it is still restrained somewhat by the fact that it is the voluntary education of adults that is under discussion. Imagine how much more passionate and divisive the battle would be if we were talking about nine year olds instead of nineteen year olds. Formal schooling is a zero-sum situation: Every hour spent on math is not spent on art; every day spent studying the internment of Japanese-Americans during World War II is not given over to the Founding Fathers or the development of tadpoles.

A program for a national curriculum is unavoidably a program for a national culture, enforced by the full authority of the state to compel schooling, and the power of the marketplace to penalize kids who are unwilling or unable to master it. For such a broad cultural redesign to be undertaken by an appointed panel working in private, as such plans typically presuppose, would violate the tenets of participatory government on which our society rests. After all, if you don't like a particular college's program of education, you can choose to go somewhere else. If the government mandates a particular national curriculum as a condition of federal aid to schools, you (unless you're pretty wealthy) can do little to escape it.

> *If you want a taste of the fury that will surround every word of the Goals 2000 curriculum, check out the attacks on the recently released American History guidelines, the first ones out of the chute and the result of three years' work by 35 national education organizations. Rush Limbaugh says they should be "flushed down the toilet". Lynne Cheney, who approved initial funding for the project as chair of the National Endowment for the Humanities, said "I feel flimflammed. These standards are really out of balance."[4] According to the Washington Post, the guidelines "have prompted some conservatives to question the need for developing national goals at all".[5]*

Some advocates of a national curriculum speak openly of a wish to promote cultural unity: As the population of the United States becomes increasingly dominated by recent immigrants from non-European countries, it becomes ever more important that all children be inculcated with a sense of what we wildly diverse Americans share. "National culture" arguments can be heard from both liberals and conservatives, the difference lying in their conception of what the national character is or ought to be.

As we discussed in chapter one, disputes over education are always disputes over who we are and who we would like to be. One of the conditions under which we hand over our children's education to the state is the right and the ability to intervene and redirect its course as necessary. This is the purpose and chief virtue of local control, and a national curriculum—by definition—removes control from the community and places it in the hands of individuals and institutions who cannot easily be held accountable.

It Talks the Talk

This denial of local control is one of the ironies of the national-curriculum movement. On the one hand, its rhetoric refers to an idyllic past of competent, dedicated teachers and students working in a strongly anchored community school. On the other, it seeks to shift authority over what goes on in schools from the community—and from teachers and staff as well —to an appointed body of "curricular experts."

> Most curricula are now designed by academics or textbook publishers who have never taught high-school students. Would you buy a car designed by an engineer who had never driven before?

On the one hand, a national curriculum calls for increased professionalism of teachers and administrators; on the other, it gives them less and less of the discretion that professionals expect and deserve. Any curriculum selection process that relies on the judgment of academic "experts" and leaves teachers, parents, and administrators out of the loop will only increase the de-skilling and de-professionalization of teaching while further alienating parents from their children's education.

On the one hand, a national curriculum calls for increased parental involvement; on the other, it removes parents even further from the loop. While it is difficult to imagine that, were citizens to be consulted, parents in rural Missouri, suburban Westchester County, and urban Los Angeles could easily agree on what a national curriculum should comprise, it is just as difficult to imagine that we would embark on this kind of project without consulting them.

According to its proponents, a national curriculum would prepare our kids for the twenty-first century. In fact, though, the establishment of a national curriculum will ensure that our educational system will respond and evolve as slowly as everything else the government does. Knowledge growth has accelerated to the point that any national curriculum would be out of step with the state of the art by the time it was implemented, and the top-heavy bureaucratic machinations involved in modifying it would consign education to a state of perpetual anti-innovation.

The trick is to answer the concerns addressed by national curriculum proposals, to distill their valuable components, in a way that preserves what we value about our quirky, decentralized, nonstandardized tradition of schooling. This is not impossible. There's no reason schools cannot offer curricula that are well thought out, assessable, and rigorous without creating a bureaucratic, inflexible, cookie-cutter system that takes parents out of the loop. The key lies in getting over our obsession with state-imposed uniformity, and in creating responsible choices for parents and administrators.

Un-American Activities

The final, greatest difficulty with a national curriculum is that it just doesn't fit well with historical American values. We don't have a state ethnicity or a state religion. We don't hold to one party line. The whole idea of America is that anyone can join, and that America comprehends a tremendous diversity of backgrounds, values, and goals. The strength of this country—what we have to offer the world—is the vision and practice of collision between all these different and competing ideas and practices. This has always been messy and difficult in practice, but it has been the source of our greatness.

A single national curriculum would not only be immensely difficult to establish in a country as diverse and culturally rich as ours, it would also be undesirable. If one of the purposes of schools is to transmit democratic values, our schools must teach these values by example. What we need is a *responsive* system, one that provides the accountability promised in theory by a rigorous national curriculum while encouraging a diversity of study that will both mirror our variety as a people and foster the ongoing educational improvement that we owe to our children and ourselves.

Every proposal for national standards presumes that (a) given a chance, people will agree on standards; (b) if they can't, they'll be comfortable with the government's decision; and (c) if they aren't, the standards could be so general that there will be plenty of room for them to stray.

The fact is, a single standard just won't work, no matter how flexible, "voluntary," or discussed. At any level of specificity, its goals would be imposed upon every student, every teacher, and every school. Even if the test is challenging, and sets difficult goals, they're someone else's goals. We *can't* all just get along. Not only is there no single curriculum that's appropriate for everyone in the country, there's none that works for an entire state or city, either. The solution isn't to be found by choosing that curriculum more carefully, or by choosing better tests for it, or by allowing some insignificant local deviation. It can only be found in encouraging the development and usage of *many* quite different curricula, each linked to its own rigorous, content–based exam. This is the only system that will promote responsiveness to community and individual needs, along with systemic accountability.

Get to the Point

2

CHAPTER 5
The Point

The Three Principles of Reform

As we've discussed, there's little agreement on whether our schools are doing a good job, though certainly the debate is dominated by people who think they are not. Almost everyone agrees that the world is changing, and that our system could be improved. We believe that meaningful reform should rest on three principles:

1. The Customers of Schools are not Students

You may think that students and parents are the customers of a school. They pay for everything and hope to benefit from the education received there. If you think this, though, you must wonder why parents and students rarely have any real say in how schools are run (whatever happened to "the customer is always right"?).

Or perhaps you think the customer of American schools is society itself. After all, our system of government and economics depends on an educated populace. We've had public schools in various forms since before we had wage labor or any colleges to speak of. But "society" pretty much lets schools slide (with occasional whining), unless there's some crisis. The abstraction of society isn't much of a customer. Society doesn't motivate people (or schools) to behave in one way or another; specific institutions, and the rewards or punishments they administer, do.

To understand how schools actually work, you should think of students not as the *customers* of schools but as their output, their *product*. High schools "sell" this product to colleges and businesses. For better or worse, people assess their communities' schools by looking at how ready kids are for college or work, not by how many register to vote. You can easily see this by watching parents evaluate schools. In wealthy suburbs, people shop for houses on the basis of the school district's college admissions record. In working-class areas, schools are judged by the percentage of the class able to get jobs upon graduation. If colleges are excited about the quality of their new students and companies are pleased to hire recent graduates, "society" shows little interest in change.

> Thinking of students as products of schools is part of the heritage of the nineteenth-century factory model. It explains a lot of the strange practices that go on around schooling: Why don't schools ask students to evaluate their teachers? Why aren't students included on curriculum or textbook review panels? To make no pretense of paying attention to your customers or investors is terrible business. But what company listens to its product? Does Hostess listen to its Twinkies? Does Tyson survey its chickens?

Colleges and businesses, then, have tremendous influence over the conduct of American education. As important customers for its product, they have a social responsibility and a selfish interest in letting schools know what capacities they desire in high-school graduates. To the extent that they neglect this responsibility, they (and we) will be stuck with an unsatisfactory product.

2. Tests and Curricula Must Be Closely Linked

People see tests as snapshots of educational progress. As we've discussed, though, tests are *targets* set for students, teachers, and administrators; they don't just assess education, but also define its content and goals.

Tests that are closely integrated with curricula, like the APs, promote good teaching. If the tests are well planned and constructed (and that's a big *if*), they set clear and reasonable goals, and measure the degree to which those goals have been met.

> You'll notice we use test and assessment *interchangeably*; though most people equate the word test with multiple-choice exams, we assume that a test might be oral, essay, performance, or anything else that can demonstrate accomplishment.

Most tests are add-ons or overlays to existing programs, however. Since they're not related to curricula in any meaningful way, they cannot address the underlying features of schools that make schools behave the way they do.

Competency tests—like those that determine whether a student is eligible for promotion—encourage teachers and students to focus on a few basics (as evaluated by a multiple-choice format). As everyone focuses on these targeted areas—and stops working on other, less rewarded, areas—performance on these tests rises while overall education suffers. Curriculum-free tests like the SAT end up replacing the curriculum itself.

3. There Must Be a Middle Ground Between Local and Central Control
It is possible that a single national curriculum could help increase accountability, but it would also impose yet another bureaucracy on our schools, suppress innovation, and bring standards to a lowest common denominator. Like other centralized education programs, it will bring about unresolvable debate every year about its content and values. Like those other programs, it will further deprofessionalize and demoralize teachers.

Absolute local control is equally problematic. Having each school set its own curriculum makes textbooks fat and unfocused for everyone. Moreover, it renders accountability impossible. Since there's no larger standard against which to judge, it's impossible to know which teachers and schools are doing a good or bad job, making performance-related proposals like merit pay and school choice almost pointless.

To some degree, the current system is the worst of both worlds. Through centralization we have made our schools drearily similar (the same courses using the same textbooks meeting for roughly the same number of hours), but just different enough to make reasonable comparison a nightmare. The national tests we use are generally so bad because they're trying to assess students in thousands of varied programs.

What we want is a system that is accountable (like a centralized system), but flexible (like a local one), a system that will allow schools to be as diverse as our communities, and encourage teachers and schools to learn from each other.

Multiple National Goals

As we've been hinting, what the U.S. needs is a system of Multiple National Curricula, whereby a school teaching American History, for example, would choose from among fifty different curricula (again, that's as opposed to writing its own or teaching to the one national curriculum). Some of these curricula might stress colonial America or the twentieth century, while others might trace threads ("religion in America") as an approach to various eras. Some would focus on the experiences of minorities, others would be more traditional.

Each curriculum would have its own nationally administered assessment, which would seek to measure the skills and knowledge that it was trying to teach, rather than such innate things as aptitude, reasoning, or intelligence. The tests would be long enough to test real content or skills and, as noted, could contain essays and short answers or take the form of interviews, demonstrations, or portfolios.

Each curriculum would come with a prospectus containing certain common-sense information: background on the authors and its goals; information on the construction and scoring of its final test; statistics on the performance of various gender, ethnic, and socioeconomic groups. This prospectus would be available before the beginning of the school year and would help teachers, students, and parents make informed choices about their classes and plan their year.

> In other words, curricula should be a little like cookies. We don't want a country in which everyone is forced to eat the same cookies. At the same time, it would be time-consuming and difficult for each family to bake its own. While some people like to bake, others seem happy with the selection of Oreos, Fig Newtons, Mrs. Fields, etc. Certainly, no one is complaining about a crisis in our ovens, a "rising tide of mediocre snacks."

In choosing the curricula that will be taught, each school (or, ideally, each teacher) would become involved in setting goals that reflect the values of its community. In describing the goals for each class, the school would help students and parents put their work in context. And since each curriculum would be taught to many different students by many different teachers in many different schools all around the country, we would finally have a reasonable means to evaluate accomplishment across the board.

How to Get There in Ten Minutes

If it were easy to change schools, one of the thousands of books about school reform (some by people ostensibly in a position to act on their ideas) would have done so.

Changing the way schools work would be like turning the largest ship in the world *if* there were a single captain and he was sure of the direction in which he wanted to turn. But for better or for worse, no one is in charge of this $260-billion-per-year machine composed of more than 100,000 schools in 15,000 districts.

To change direction, to create coherent reform at the deep structural level, we need a long lever: a person or a group of people who can catalyze the entire educational community, who can make it clear that the advantages of buying into change are exceeded only by the costs of staying behind. In basketball, the key to an offense is the player at the point (the center of the court, behind the foul line). In education, as in basketball, the key is the pointman. And we believe this pointman must be an important *customer* of the high-school product—someone who runs a leading college.

Colleges, through their admissions requirements, have the power to determine what goes on in American classrooms. Unlike the federal government, they can set those requirements without votes or public debate; after all, who is going to tell them how they should choose their students?

The Pointman

That's why the President of Harvard University can revolutionize American education *right now*. All he has to do is get on television and make a simple announcement: As of the year 2002, Harvard will change its admissions policies. In addition to grades, the college will require students to submit their scores on nationally administered assessments for each subject in high school. Depending on the course of study that a student pursued in high school, that might mean as many as twenty tests over four years.

The college would accept a variety of curricula and assessments. In other words, Harvard would endorse a curriculum by accepting its linked test as a partial fulfillment of admissions requirements. To earn that endorsement, a curriculum would have to meet certain standards, including the following:

- The new tests will be closely tied to curricula, and administered nationally under controlled conditions.

- The tests and curricula will have to be reasonably rigorous, fair, and open. Students and parents will be given detailed information to help them understand the goals and philosophy of the various curricula before they enrolled in their courses. Under our proposal, Harvard will not dictate the content of the curriculum.

- The data from the tests will have to be available to researchers. (As we'll see, that data will become an important part of our proposal.)

- Harvard will encourage the development and refinement of new curricula by any interested parties, who will be, in effect, the sponsors of those curricula. Harvard will encourage schools to offer varied and differing selections from among them.

This may seem somewhat anticlimactic. How could we change the entire educational system by tinkering with Harvard's admissions requirements? Perhaps you thought the one person who could change American education would be an elected official or a terrorist. Stay with us.

Perched at the end of a very long lever, Harvard is perhaps the institution in the single best position to change our educational system (though, ideally, it would act in concert with other prestigious universities). As you'll see over the next few chapters, each of the other players in education, acting entirely in its own self-interest, will fall in line from here. In effect, Harvard can bring about change not through brute force or even moral suasion, but just by setting certain wheels in motion.

Pointpeople

It's possible that Harvard will have no interest in changing its requirements for admission. It may be that Harvard is perfectly satisfied with the quality of the applicants it now gets, and has no real wish to get involved in meaningful school reform. While it would be a powerful engine in the drive for change, certainly there are others who could act to get things rolling.

For example, other Ivy League schools could get together to make the same statement. So could the Big 10 schools, the California University system, or an alliance of liberal arts colleges. The National Association of College Admissions Counselors (NACAC) could vote to support this. Even ETS (who writes the SAT) or the College Board (who sponsors it) could decide that it would be better for them to replace the SAT than to have some other company get there first.

Although elite colleges are in the best position to start things rolling, Multiple National Curricula will ultimately be as applicable to high schools that send most students to the job market as to those who send 100 percent to selective colleges.

It doesn't really matter who the pointman is. The key is that some institution currently involved in college admissions must realize that it has the power to change American schools, and then have the will and the courage to move forward.

Curricula and Tests

There is nothing unique about trying to improve education by linking it to a new kind of test. We did not write this book just to propose new college-admissions requirements. Our agenda is to add a degree of accountability to schools while also encouraging flexibility. To seek accountability without flexibility is to ignore the best classroom teaching.

Under our plan, a teacher would commit to following a particular curriculum, and using its test. That means that he or she would, at the start of a semester, commit to covering particular material to an agreed-upon depth of understanding. Administrators, students, and parents would know at the outset what the expectations were for the course.

The curricular selection process for each school would, ideally, be an open collaboration between faculty, staff, and interested parents. Sponsors or proponents of various curricula would be given a forum to lobby for their favored programs. The school English department might advocate one literature curriculum, the State Office of Education another, the PTA another, and a conservative religious group yet another. Since different schools and districts will have different governance policies, those responsible for making the final determination on curricula might or might not be required to take the wishes of all these groups into account. Depending upon its resources and the wishes of its constituents, a school might, for instance, offer six English, five social studies, two biology, and four music courses to its students, or it might offer only one of each.

Whatever the selection process, though, a teacher committing to teach a particular curriculum would also be committing to the assessment that comes with it. A curriculum might be so specific as to suggest particular modes of teaching and specific classroom exercises, or it might simply indicate its goals and leave the rest to the teacher. All curricula, however, would end with some measure of the success of the class in achieving those goals. With these crucial factors held constant across many different classroom settings, it will become possible to see what other ingredients in the learning mix—class size, teaching style, choice of textbook, and so on—add value and which do not. At the end of the term, the curriculum–linked exam will serve to judge students' performance against that of other students all across the country who have used the same curriculum.

Authority and Accountability

In business, a new employee generally clears every important decision with her boss, but is not held responsible for success or failure. As she rises in the company, she gains more authority to make independent decisions, and at the same time is held increasingly responsible for their success or failure: Authority and accountability are thus closely coupled.

If by "accountability" we mean a responsibility for success and failure that has consequences attached to it, then public education lacks it almost completely. Few students are ever held back because they fail to reach predefined goals. A teacher's or principal's salary or career path is not much affected by the performance of the students in his charge, and it's almost unheard of for schools to be closed for consistently failing to educate their kids, no matter how grievous, widespread, and long–standing the shortfall might be.

This lack of accountability, this inability to require that performance standards be met, has encouraged administrators and politicians to pull authority from teachers and principals. Since there is no way to know if they're doing a good job or not, the thinking goes, it's best to make school workers follow as closely as possible a uniform set of guidelines determined by higher–ups. Teachers are forced to follow and file lesson plans, and are paid according to seniority rather than performance. Unless they have special waivers, principals are required by law to organize learning according to the cookie-cutter prototype the state specifies for every school. The more aggressive and innovative a principal is, the less likely he is to be rewarded with long tenure in the system. In this light the profession of education looks less and less like a profession at all.

Under the Multiple National Curriculum plan, teachers (and, by extension, principals) are judged by their students' achievement. Since many students across the country will be taking the same test at the end of the year, it should be possible to determine with far greater confidence the contribution made by a particular teacher. To some degree, we will know who is doing a good job and who is not. Teachers and principals will, for the first time, be subjected to the kinds of close, ongoing scrutiny we have always reserved for students, as if students were solely responsible for their own outcomes.

Holding people accountable without giving them the freedom to achieve their objectives in their own way makes no sense. You can't take someone to task for poor performance if you've forced them to perform in a certain way from the start. Teachers are right to resist the proposals like merit pay that make them accountable without giving them the freedom to actually be different from one another in order to improve and excel.

Given the swift and certain accountability afforded by the Multiple National Curricula plan, it makes sense to treat teachers and administrators as the professionals that our rhetoric makes them out to be. That means encouraging them to get involved in both the design and the selection of curricula they will teach. It means allowing them to organize their classrooms and schools as they think best, knowing that their successes and failures will be reflected in their students' performance at the end of the year. Unlike most testing programs, ours will take neither spontaneity nor authority from the classroom. On the contrary, it will encourage risk-taking and innovation by educators who want to excel, and eliminate the need for bureaucrats far removed from the complex realities of the classroom to second–guess and micro–manage what teachers themselves know best how to do.

> We've discussed our proposal with enough teachers to duck here. We're not saying that teachers are solely responsible for their students' performance. We're not saying that a final exam, no matter how well-constructed, can possibly measure all the learning that might have occurred in the class. However, it's undeniable that you can learn a great deal by comparing students from similar backgrounds on tests that are closely tied to curricula.

100% Content-Free

Multiple National Curricula is a structural plan, an architecture. As such, it is indifferent to content. It works just as well (and just the same) whether a particular curriculum takes a Great Books, a Christian fundamentalist, or an Afrocentric approach to its subject. We'd be delighted to see national curricula for things like Creationism and Managing a 7-Eleven (though it would remain to be seen which schools would offer them and which colleges or businesses would accept them).

It is not that such differences are unimportant; on the contrary, what a plan of study seeks to convey should determine everything else—teaching style, resources, assessment—that specifically characterizes the program, since these all exist only in support of underlying curricular goals. The Multiple National Curricula plan allows such important choices between values and content to be made more rationally and more honestly by insisting that each curriculum declare itself plainly and reveal its goals, its methods, and its results.

The Multiple National Curricula plan thus enables us to distinguish performance in a given curriculum from the content and the values of the

> Under this plan, an important function of the state office of education would be the oversight of representations made about curricula in the prospectus or public forums. Any program that misrepresented itself or its sponsors would be subject to strong sanctions. There would be no stealth curricula that attempt to pass on hidden or mischaracterized agendæ for learning.

curriculum. If similar groups of students do equally well on a particular test, or in college, or on any other agreed-upon measure—regardless of whether their curriculum used books or videotapes to deliver instruction, had twelve or twenty students per class, assigned one or ten hours of homework each week, emphasized European authors or did not—then those things are probably not related to performance. If one group (e.g., the students in smaller classes) *does* excel, then we should teach others the way that we taught them. This would add at least some measure of rationality to the passionate and pointless debates about what works in the classroom.

Rather than imposing one single set of educational, social, or political values on diverse communities, the Multiple National Curricula model instead creates a structure that allows these communities to make articulated choices between real alternatives. It embraces community and professional autonomy in formulating and making those choices, encourages participation and debate among all interested parties, and provides for responsiveness and accountability at each step of the decision–making and the teaching and learning process.

Is This a National Curriculum?

At first glance, the Multiple National Curricula plan, counting as it does on the deployment of dozens of different curricula (created by dozens of different companies) for each high-school subject area, seems about as far from a single national curriculum or national test as you can get. But we believe it provides the chief advantages of a national curriculum—letting students, parents, and others know in advance what will be taught, providing reliable indicators as to how well it's been learned, and instituting accountability for schools and teachers—without the baggage that must always accompany such plans.

This model provides a mechanism by which teachers can become meaningfully involved in setting goals for their students, and gives them autonomy and flexibility in working with their students to achieve them. It keeps government out of the curriculum industry. Instead, it encourages schools, teachers, colleges, parents and test companies to go out and create—separately or in partnership— the curricula they'd like to see, and textbook companies to compete against one another to produce the best possible educational resources to support those curricula. Unlike every other proposal for a national curriculum or assessment, the Multiple National Curricula plan is flexible, adaptive to future needs, and resistant to political pressures.

CHAPTER 6

The
Domino
Effect

Critical Mass

At this point we've spelled out the fundamentals of the structure we'd like to create: Lots of independent organizations creating hundreds of national curricula, with each school choosing from among them. Students, teachers, and schools are judged by students' scores on the assessments that accompany each of the curricula (but only in part; there are plenty of important ways to look at schools besides academic performance) .

To get there, we've proposed a reform route which may seem odd. It involves no government action, and we seem to be talking about the one demographic—upper-middle class—that *least* needs help. In fact, all we have so far is one college changing its admissions criteria. This hardly seems like a revolution in education. Before anything can happen, the other players in secondary education—state agencies, testing companies, teachers, parents, other colleges, high schools, and textbook publishers—have to get on board.

In this chapter, we'll step through the process by which they will get drawn into the new system. We're not assuming any altruism on the part of any of the participants. It is simply in the (differing) self–interest of each group to work for the plans' success; as each acts, it will create a momentum behind these changes that is revolutionary.

This is not to say that those players don't care about education or don't want to see reform, but there is inertia in any institution this large and long–standing. There are reasons why so many reform efforts have failed, and why so many good ideas have had so little impact on most schools. Just as the current system depends on a set of interlocking self–interests to maintain itself, so the Multiple National Curricula proposal is also a system, with each piece serving to reinforce the overall structure. This time, though, the goal is the ongoing infusion of information, innovation, and improvement rather than an attempt to impose uniformity or insulate schools from their constituents.

As you read this, you'll probably be struck by the basic disruptions that the Multiple National Curriculum proposal will create. This is by design: we want to take the system down to the joists and rebuild from there.

The Other Colleges

Ideally, the President of Harvard would consult with many other college presidents before making his speech. The greater the number of selective colleges involved in presenting the new standards, the more difficult it will be to ignore them. Whether he has or not, however, we believe that other colleges will eventually accept his new admissions criteria.

First, they will get involved because it's the Right Thing to Do: at top colleges, a newly hired president's first statement is usually that he or she hopes to apply the expertise of the faculty to the nation's social and educational problems (the second statement generally concerns fund-raising). If college presidents and admissions officers believe that they can personally make a difference in secondary education, they will likely do so.

Second, schools that attract significant numbers of out–of–state students have a particular interest in tools that help them evaluate curricula from around the country. Most admissions people can't stand the SAT; they use it for lack of an alternative. This plan represents a chance to replace it with something that is both more flexible and a better predictor of college performance.

Third, no college wants to limit its pool of

The U.S. spends $100 million a year taking and preparing for the SAT, which is supposed to predict college performance. Yet SAT scores correlate terribly to college grades, and only slightly (.35) to freshman year grades. To make its numbers look reasonable, ETS must manipulate the data. Despite comparing a computed GPA (in which a ninth grade art class is weighted identically to an eleventh grade algebra) to an optimized blend of math and verbal SAT scores, ETS must still admit that the GPA is a better predictor of freshman year grades than is the SAT.

qualified applicants. In an era of declining enrollments and rising costs, it is difficult to imagine a college admissions officer saying "Well, this is clearly a strong applicant, she really wants to go here, and she can afford our $25,000 tuition. But we'll reject her because she took the wrong test." It's likely they will accept virtually any curricula used by significant numbers of students and schools (remember—they have to wade through an infinite number of curricula now), while rejecting students they feel learned little—for whatever reason.

Finally, colleges will accept the new tests because it will make them appear more selective and put them in the same company as the highly selective schools that accept the new assessments. This is nothing new: More than 3,000 colleges require SAT or ACT scores, even though under 300 of them are selective enough to reject even half of their applicants.

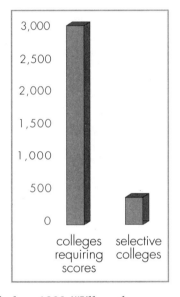

This is the dark secret of admissions hurdles like the SAT. While they are popularly thought of as a tool by which colleges choose high-school students (and the College Board would encourage you to think so), it's much more often the reverse. Students apply mainly to colleges whose average incoming scores are near their own. If you scored 1100 on the SAT, you won't bother applying to schools with average scores over 1250 ("I'll never get in") nor to schools with averages below 1000 ("I'll go there if I don't get in anywhere else").

Colleges work hard to make themselves look as selective as possible in order to attract the best students. Emory, for example, gives large scholarships to attract students with high test scores. Buying these students has helped raise its average incoming scores, which has in turn pushed college guides to change its rank from "selective" to "highly selective." This, of course, has attracted more high-scoring students. New College of South Florida and Duke University successfully raised their standards in the same way.

Even the most prestigious schools rely on stu-

Many colleges manipulate the data on the average incoming scores of their students. Savvy admissions officers often try to "NIP" those students whose scores would lower the average. In admissions lingo, "NIP" means Not In Profile—a student who has been excluded from the count, probably because he or she is an athlete, the child of an alumnus, or a member of an under-represented minority group.

dent self–selection to deliver applicants. One reason that many colleges with high incoming SAT scores can say these scores are not really an important part of their decision, and that they will look past weak scores if a candidate is compelling, is that students with weak scores don't even bother to apply.

The Multiple National Curricula plan won't do away with this behavior. We mention it only to demonstrate that colleges tend to adopt practices that enhance their image, and adopting Multiple National Curricula will do just that. If a few prestigious schools adopt our plan, most others will follow out of a combination of idealism and self–interest. Many will undoubtedly hedge their bets, accepting both the SAT and the new tests. A few might demand both, claiming that each gives important information. The reality of the college admissions marketplace, however, is that a few prestigious universities and large state schools essentially define the game. If they define a *new* game, those schools that don't play will quickly become relegated to the backwaters, and they know it.

Some people have asked if this system is too complicated for college admissions offices. Used to dealing with only one or two sets of tests, they'll now have to understand the innards of hundreds of different tests in many subjects. This is actually easier than it sounds. Every college admissions office uses computer software to keep track of and evaluate students. It will be pretty simple to teach the software the statistics and demographics of the various tests, and create a system for comparing performances of two students who took different programs all through school.

There's actually one more reason colleges should embrace the plan, though we hesitate to mention it. As things stand, college and high-school admissions officers are an endangered species. As schools cut their budgets, and colleges try to hold tuition increases down, counselors are an inviting target. Replacing admissions professionals with clerks and computers doesn't hurt student:teacher ratios or mean that the grass doesn't get cut. Over the past ten years, we've watched as most of the best counselors we know have left the field or gone into private practice.

By taking the reins of school reform, admissions people can become central players in education, instead of waiting for their inevitable pink slips. College admissions officers evaluate curricula for a living; together with department heads, this is the chance to put their skill to work for an important new cause. On the high school side, counselors will become the conduits between teachers choosing curricula and colleges evaluating them.

Many Paths

While each college will accept most curricula, each will also exercise some discretion that reflects the school's particular approach to education and the opinions of faculty in its various departments. But as a given curriculum finds favor with a few colleges, others will be pressured to accept it too. For example, once the University of Michigan accepts a particular chemistry course, Michigan State is very likely to follow. The state university systems, which in each state attract the majority of college–bound students, will carry the flag of Multiple National Curricula into their respective states, further encouraging its adoption by their public high schools. In this way a series of individual, voluntary decisions can put a national system into place without any national edicts being issued. This is the same type of leverage that permits a few states with textbook–selection policies to control the textbook market of the entire country. Under the Multiple National Curriculum plan, however, that leverage is used to pry markets open and encourage diversity, rather than to foreclose it.

This pressure to accept many curricula is a good thing. The Multiple National Curricula plan will work best if the greatest number of curricula are introduced by as many different groups as possible—especially in the early years—so that everyone can see the advantages and disadvantages of each. The legitimation function performed by the decisions of colleges will be more productive when it embraces than when it excludes. Although we don't want colleges to abrogate their responsibility to exercise judgment in this area, neither do we want them to be the sole arbiter of what constitutes good curricula. Rather, they should be an integral component of a responsive system that ultimately considers the judgments of teachers, parents, students, the job market, and policy makers to be equally important. Since the acceptance of a broad range of curricula is demonstrably in the colleges' own interests, it seems likely that it will, in fact, turn out this way.

Clearly, there's a danger that colleges will get together to judge curricula through an organization like The College Board. Although this would make the world easier for the colleges, it could lessen the pressure on them to accept innovations and diversity. We'll return to this issue.

Testing the Testers

An announcement by the top colleges will create, of course, a tremendous opportunity for the testing companies, who will waste no time jumping into the fray. They will team up with potential curriculum sponsors–people with strong feelings about what should be taught–to create the new test/ curriculum combinations that everyone insists we *not* call *testicula*.

When they create curricula, the sponsors will have to please two clients. The first are the colleges, who will have to sign on to new curricula and their accompanying assessments; the second and tougher group will be the schools. At least initially, those new curricula that are successful will probably have started with a strong base of clients and build from there. This base might be constituted by associations like the Coalition for Essential Schools, single–sex prep schools, or the schools of a particular state. But any institution, group, or individual could design and sponsor a curriculum, submitting it to schools and colleges for approval.

Many of the new tests and curricula produced under the Multiple National Curricula plan will be quite mainstream in their appeal. They will be similar to one another and to the most polished of the current efforts. Others, though, will be more experimental, or appeal to smaller niches. Some would target inner–city schools while others might address students at Jesuit schools or schools that teach the Great Books.

The first of these mainstream assessments might well look something like the College Board's Advanced Placement (AP) tests. These are nationally administered and curriculum–based, each about three hours long. They're integrated with an AP curriculum, which is usually the toughest taught by a school, far more rigorous than honors courses. Though they contain some multiple-choice questions, the exams are not shallow; they contain essays and short-answer questions, and most teachers and students feel they require more than just a knowledge of dates and places. As with our proposed tests, APs are generally administered as the final exam in an AP course, so most classroom time is spent teaching, not testing.

But as we've noted, many of the new assessments would look nothing like the AP. Some curricula might require a performance, an essay done over a week, or an oral exam. Some might involve creating a portfolio. Some tests might be given on a computer or over a video link; as the technologies change, the instruments will change with them. Our proposal is not about tests *per se*; it's about assessment. Anything that gives a relatively consistent measure of what a student has (or hasn't) learned is fine.

Some of the new curricula will be designed to teach content, while others teach skills. But all of them are very likely teaching something whose assimilation by students is measurable in some way.

Tighter Textbooks

The textbook companies, too, will jump right in. Writing a textbook that corresponds to a particular test and curriculum should be much simpler than writing a one-size-fits-all tome through which each teacher picks a path. Instead of differentiating their products with full–color photographs and other fluff, textbook companies will produce truly distinctive editions of their books specially tailored to particular courses of study.

This fits well into the trend towards "custom publishing" that is reshaping the college-textbook market. Many college professors now give chapters from many different books to the bookstore or a local copy center. When they assign a reading to the class, the students buy copies of the chapters (the copy center remits a licensing fee to the appropriate publisher). The students get a "textbook" geared to the course they're taking, and information providers (publishers) get paid based on the amount of information bought. The rise of custom publishing suggests the pent-up demand for textbooks that are tailored to the needs of a class.

> *Right now, these custom-published books look like, well, a pile of photocopies. But recent technical advances make it possible to produce high-quality bound books, on very short notice, in this way. And as libraries become more and more accessible over an increasingly robust information infrastructure, it will become trivial to have students download material on an as–needed basis. The inexpensive storage of thousands of these documents in central servers will constitute a toolbox of components for an entire series of flexible, refinable "virtual textbooks." This is already a familiar practice at many universities, with professors placing electronic copies of papers and articles on a central server for students to download as needed.*

Will High Schools Jump Too?

This is where our proposal is most severely tested. Why will high schools agree to use these tests? This new world institutes an accountability that is surely unnerving to many of the people who will find themselves under public evaluation for the first time. Further, school systems have a track record of resistance to almost every meaningful education initiative of the past sixty years.

And yet the schools will line up behind this new structure, and will, within a few years, choose, develop, and promote curricula that are varied and rigorous.

The first schools to switch will be the high–end prep schools that send bunches of kids to Ivy League colleges. These are generally good schools with little to fear from the accountability that this proposal brings. Most of their students will score well on these new tests, whatever they are. Prep schools have long been governed by one of the plan's central premises— that selective colleges are important clients, and that high schools are most meaningfully judged by their success at meeting their clients' needs and expectations. Early acceptance of Multiple National Curricula will give these schools real input into what is taught and measured by the first set of curricula, and a chance to build a base of support for the curricula they currently use. Further, these schools (whose teachers and administrators are typically paid far less than their counterparts in the public schools) might discover a new source of revenue in the production of instructional materials and training workshops for other schools.

As the private schools come into the system, the pressure will next fall on the suburban public schools, just as elite private colleges led the way for the elite public universities. Parents at these schools are very concerned about college admissions and about the relative performance of their schools; many moved to their communities because of the schools. However, these public schools are not free to single–handedly switch their curricula, bound as they are by state rules and procedures (e.g., graduation requirements or adoption of textbooks).

Ideally, states will continue the trend of granting waivers to schools or districts seeking to pursue their own policies, as Massachusetts, Michigan, and nine other states do for their charter schools. Such autonomy would facilitate the ability of public schools to embrace the Multiple National Curricula as one possible response to the needs of their constituents. Even without that autonomy, though, public schools could embrace the Multiple National Curricula, should they wish to do so. In many subject areas, the most general or commonplace curricula proposed will be similar to the states' existing guidelines, and little change to current teaching practices will be necessary. Should the state's requirements for an acceptable curriculum differ significantly from all those that are extant, a curriculum developer will undoubtedly be willing to mold a new curriculum and test in the form required to meet the Multiple National Curriculum standards, and get the colleges to accept it as such.

Statewide Adoption

The general notion of holding schools to standards has always been politically popular; a misapplication of that instinct is part of what got us into this mess in the first place. Faced with pressure from above and below—the top colleges rallying behind this plan and the demands for school reform building from their constituents—school officials may find that the path of least resistance is to adopt one or more of the national curricula and assessments for their own schools. This is the edge of the wedge: In time, a great number of nationally accepted and closely followed curricula will foster accountability for schools, nonintrusive, nonprescriptive oversight by states and the federal government, and meaningful local control. Under this plan, a state could allow schools to pick (within boundaries that can be as broad or as narrow as its citizens demand) what works for them.

It could, for instance, decide to hold all of its schools to a single curriculum for each subject. By doing so, it would lose the social and pedagogical advantages of a diverse set of curricula, but still gain the advantages of having national performance standards. Parents would know what their kids were expected to learn and be able to hold schools responsible for their role in that process. Policy makers at the district and state levels would have access to greater amounts of high–quality information about what specific schools were doing.

A more productive scenario would be for a state to bless two or more of the curricula that would rapidly emerge, and allow its schools to teach any or all of them. The state would still approve the curricula from which schools could choose, and could still set graduation requirements—four years of any approved English curricula; three years of any approved science curricula; three years of any approved arts curricula, and so forth—yet shift the power to determine the course of study, back to the local level.

> In a world of Multiple National Curricula, the meaning of "teacher training" would be very different. It's likely that teachers would be involved in selecting the curricula they teach, and that they would work with many different curricula during their careers. Basic teacher education, therefore, would best consist of preparing teachers to evaluate different apparatus to teaching and learning, and help inculcate a flexible and adaptive attitude toward developing knowledge and skills in students. With this as a base, and given teachers who are knowledgeable in their fields, it's doubtful that the specific training for even the most dramatically innovative curriculum would need to be longer than a few weeks.

The state could continue to set standards for teacher certification, but a significant proportion of that training would become increasingly systematized, subsidized, and conducted by the curriculum developers, of which the state would likely be one among many.

Adopting Large Families

The most interesting iteration would be one in which states accept almost every curriculum, returning full choice of what and how to teach to the districts and schools themselves. All curricula accepted by that state's college system would be certified regardless of content or philosophy, and most teacher certification requirements would be dropped. While this would no doubt lead to a few "bad" curricula being embraced by some schools for a while, ultimately the data generated on the correlation of particular curricula with success in college or the job market will weed out those that fail to serve their clients. Even in a worst–case scenario, the damage inflicted on schools that happen to adopt what later turns out to be a flawed course of study will be less than that caused by mistakes made under the current system. Since the decision is a local one made only at one or a few schools, it doesn't affect the majority of schools that did not choose that curriculum. Under the present system, by contrast, the drive towards uniformity in schooling leads to decisions whose consequences are far more global. When a state sets misguided "standards" *all* its schools suffer.

Regardless of which of the preceding broad scenarios a state follows, it could also become involved in the development of curricula to suit its particular policy objectives and constraints: curricula for schools with limited funds; antidrug curricula; curricula that support strategic industries; curricula for schools with a high teacher-turnover rate, and so on. With a private partner willing to champion the new curriculum to the colleges and administer it on a national level, good examples of these state–sponsored curricula could themselves become national standards.

Which of these scenarios develops depends on specific policy decisions about how far to go with decentralization. It seems unlikely that many states will feel comfortable giving up all their standard–setting authority. Most voters want the state to oversee and certify, at least to some extent, what their kids are taught. We expect that many states would initially allow only a few curricula at most in each subject area, but would eventually come under pressure to allow more. This scalability, the capacity to ramp up autonomy as it's earned, gives everyone a chance to get comfortable with the new landscape and to develop the skills necessary to make it work.

Despite initial discomfort, schools will quickly benefit from these changes, and do a better job with students. The potential for states to shift significant numbers of dollars from standards–setting bureaucracies into the classroom will mean more money to pay competitive salaries, maintain physical plants, and stay on top of new technologies. Perhaps most important, the people who work in schools can begin to be regarded—and to function—as true professionals.

The Prospectus

In order for a test and curriculum to be acceptable under our proposed guidelines, students and parents would have to be informed of the goals of each course in great detail before it started. We believe this is an important benefit of the plan, one best implemented through a curriculum prospectus.

Just as an investment prospectus follows a detailed template to inform potential investors or buyers about the company or property they are considering, every curriculum should make available a booklet that lays out in plain language what the curriculum is trying to accomplish, why it feels those goals are important, and how it intends to achieve them. It should include a sample test that supports what the sponsors believe to be the spirit and goals of the curriculum. For those assessments that involve some type of multimedia portfolio or presentation, representative samples should be available at the school (eventually, it will be easy and inexpensive to download these on demand). A few years after their introduction, prospectuses would begin to be updated yearly to include performance and demographic data on the students and schools that follow it (more on this in chapter seven).

The test should be accompanied by some statistics about the scores of the students who have taken them. What is average? What is a "good" score? How do various minority groups score? In other words, as you look at this curriculum, how much of it can you expect your son or daughter will actually learn?

Once the basic reporting requirements are met, the prospectus can be as specific or as general as its sponsors wish. It might describe in great detail what students will cover each week and provide teachers with detailed lesson plans, handouts, and homework assignments, or it might affirm in only the most general terms that students who complete the program are expected to have a working knowledge of, say, the novel and essay form as practiced in eighteenth–century England, and be able to demonstrate it in a thousand–word critical essay.

It's critical that colleges, states, and schools require sponsors of curricula to provide such a prospectus to parents and students. If we are going to institute accountability, it would be bizarre to keep the rules from the participants. The information would already exist, since it's unlikely that a proposal that did not spell out these rudiments would have much chance of approval. Making this information available to parents and students will be both logical and inexpensive.

The Business Community

Nearly every national business and professional association has taken an official position on school reform. Some send representatives to high–level policy coalitions like the Business Roundtable to formulate fairly detailed recommendations for specific state action. Within states and local communities, business leaders, as perceived customers of schools' output, often have substantial influence on the goals and directions that schools adopt. Historically, their influence can be seen in the rise of vocational education and "business math" classes.

> That's not to say that businesses should be running the schools. Your dissatisfaction with a school does not qualify you to run it.

Some professions like engineering require a steady stream of students who are well prepared within specific disciplines. Others, including traditionally blue–collar trades, claim to want students who are able to work well together in teams, think and work independently and flexibly, and feel comfortable in a problem–solving role. Some, like telephone or mail-order companies and others who work directly with the public, simply want people who show up on time, take direction easily, and can speak and write standard English.

The Multiple National Curricula plan gives all these groups an opportunity to make tangible contributions to our educational system by designing or blessing specific curricula that meet their needs. Boeing, for example, might design an aviation mechanics curriculum and an aeronautical engineering program that would be available for adoption nationwide. Such curricula would probably involve apprenticeship as an integral component, and its assessment might include the design of an airfoil or a hydraulic circuit. A particular score on the Boeing test would indicate that the student was qualified to perform certain kinds of work (if for no one else, then at least for Boeing) and think through problems in a particular body of knowledge.

Industries and professions could scale their involvement in curricular involvement to reflect their needs, their resources, and their commitment to education. Under the Multiple National Curricula plan, it will become increasingly difficult for businesses to complain about the state of education without offering their own substantive contribution.

Competition and Chaos

As testing companies and curriculum developers compete to sign up schools and colleges for their tests, as schools pick the curricula by which they will be judged, as colleges pick the tests they will accept, and as textbook companies try to figure out which curricula will create large markets for support materials and which would be a waste of time, we expect to see a few years of jockeying.

If high schools are passive during this period then the structure and momentum of the education "market" will allow colleges and curriculum developers to play the major role in determining which courses are actually available for teaching. That would be a mistake. Schools will have the opportunity—and should have the incentive—to gain a significant amount of self–determination through participation in the curriculum development and selection process. It makes sense for them to seek this, since their successes or failures at teaching the new curricula will become a matter of public record. Most importantly, as the entities closest to the learning process, schools have a particular responsibility to act as a counter–balance to the market forces that might otherwise prevail against the best interests of students and learning. The key to the success of the Multiple National Curriculum plan here, as in other areas, is the mix of synergy and tension between the self–interests of all the participants.

By the time the class of 2002 gets to high school, most of the pieces should be in place, with dozens of registered curricula for each high school subject (more of such popular courses as math or English; fewer for subjects like Latin or economics). Each of those curricula will be accompanied by a final exam, which will be nationally administered and scored. Almost every college will accept these tests in lieu of the SAT or ACT. Depending on how each state decides to structure the curriculum selection process, each school might be teaching some unique combination of curricula—a school might teach French in just one way, but have three of four different algebra curricula—or the same subset as every other school in its state. When students pick their classes for the following term, they'll review curriculum prospectuses describing each one, which will serve as their road map for the semester. Any materials the school provides for use during the year, and any materials the students buy to help supplement their studies, will be geared to their courses (see chapter eight).

At this point, we'll be through the painful part of the process. Even if it went no further, the Multiple National Curricula model would be a significant improvement over both the current state of education and the proposals for its future direction. It would avert a restrictive top–down national curriculum or testing program while moving the schools toward a new level of accountability and responsiveness. But as soon as the numbers start coming in, things will really get interesting.

CHAPTER 7

Full
and Fair
Disclosure

Good Information

Education currently takes place in a fog. No one has the information needed to make informed decisions. Parents have only a vague idea what schools are doing with their kids and how well they're doing it. Teachers have only their gut instinct to tell them if a tool (software, textbook, video) is helping their students or not. Administrators have no way of fairly judging their teachers—one of the absurdities of introducing merit pay under the current regime. Voters have no way of knowing whether cutting back on school spending will improve efficiency or destroy their schools. Researchers seldom accept the validity of one another's studies because of the inherent problems with experimental design when evaluating something like educational outcome.

Such perpetual ignorance would be intolerable in medicine, business, science, or even sports ("Well, we think our team is doing fine. We've played ten games this year, and enjoyed all of them. We're looking forward to 'bat left–handed' day."). Why then should we accept it in our educational system, whose very mission is to fight ignorance?

Past attempts to discover what works best in the classroom and why it works have been plagued by a lack of good information. Teachers, parents, and students have much direct experience of what works for them, but little way of knowing how applicable it might be to other classrooms, subjects, or social environments. On top of this, they're seldom asked to share their experience with others in a systematic way. The Multiple National Curricula plan provides a framework within which to compare the performance of students, teachers, schools, states, textbooks, and high–level policies by consistent, content–linked yardsticks. Just as important, it provides for the aggressive, consequential dissemination of the results so that everyone can learn from everyone else's experience.

The point of all this data is not only to find out where the best textbooks, teachers, or schools are, but to give us a mechanism to replicate good work and disseminate information about the best current practices in education. For years, we've been squandering the most valuable benefits of our aggregate educational experience.

Garbage In, Garbage Out

A major roadblock to educational accountability and the increased autonomy that should accompany it has been this difficulty in collecting good information and getting it to parents and administrators in a form they can use. Although reams of statistics are collected about schools, teachers, and students, and a great deal of fuss made over the publication of state-average SAT scores, or district–by–district reading levels, it makes little discernible difference.

This is largely because the type of information that's currently being collected rarely supports the educational standards our society claims to hold. Standardized tests do a poor job at measuring the higher–order thinking skills we now claim to wish for our students. State or national tests that seek to measure knowledge of history or competence in math are seldom closely tied to what kids actually study in school, and so tend to reflect what is or isn't being taught rather than what is or isn't being learned. Since the SAT makes no attempt to measure what students learn in high school, having school districts compete against one another on the basis of SAT scores serves no discernible educational purpose and detracts from the teaching of authentic, important content and learning skills.

Second, when information about school effects is reported now, it's as an isolated outcome, with little background on the many factors that contributed to producing it. A reading score, for instance, tells you nothing about the number of kids in the class, the years of experience of the teacher, how much and what type of homework is assigned, and what method is used to instruct the kids. The same can be said for scores on the majority of state–mandated tests, even those that, like the New York State Regents exams, are quite good at testing meaningful learning.

Third, while a few states—notably Massachusetts and Minnesota—are starting to release performance information broken down to the school level, the data that tends to get the most publicity is limited to the district or state level, and does not extend to the individual school or classroom. This means that parents and community groups rarely know what's going on in the particular schools that concern them. People are naturally more interested in the quality of their children's schools than with that of schools in general, and so the aggregate information that is released holds little meaning and less value for them. To understand just how absurd this situation is, compare the amount and detail of information that's available to help us make trivial recreational decisions about sports, movies, and restaurants with what's available on the institutions to whom we largely entrust our children's intellectual development.

> A notable exception: Massachusetts' recently created School District Profiles do a fine job of sharing what information does exist in a readable format.

The Multiple National Curriculum proposal establishes a mechanism to remedy this, to ensure that useful information is generated and disseminated in a timely and reliable manner. And it does so without creating expensive new regulatory burdens on taxpayers or schools.

Honest Packaging and Sausage

We believe that reliable, detailed information on the results obtained by schools and teachers using identifiable curricula, assessments, and materials is a necessary precursor to both greater accountability and greater autonomy. This is the only rational way to get the kind of practical information that can advance teaching, learning, and administration. It is the only fair way to begin a classroom–level scrutiny of student achievement.

At the same time, the availability of that information should encourage everyone involved in education—from students, to principals, to textbook writers—to produce his or her best work. We hope to provide a framework under which large and small developers vie to create tests and curricula that colleges will accept and schools will teach. Designers of instructional materials will compete against one another to tailor textbooks and other materials to each curriculum, and will be judged by the success of schools and teachers who use them. Having chosen a given curriculum (for example, the Smithsonian American History Program), schools, teachers, and students will compete to best teach and learn that curriculum.

But the integrity of the entire system relies on the quality of the information available to all participants at every step. Only if the data is rigorously collected and aggressively distributed can parents, teachers, students, schools, and colleges evaluate curricula and instruction. This is no different than for any of the market–based mechanisms on which we depend in other aspects of our lives. You need more than a good price and a nice brochure to make an informed judgment. You choose a car after looking at things like safety features and repair history. You try to buy foods that are good for you. You vote for a president after examining his experience and positions. In every case, you judge competing products or candidates against a reference point that is either personal (your political philosophy), generally accepted (minimum daily nutritional requirements) or a combination of both (the trade–off between acceleration and crash survivability).

We take this kind of comparison shopping for granted in many, if not most, areas of our lives, and our systems of government and economics assume it as a condition of doing the jobs we ask of them. A functioning market of products, services, or ideas depends upon everyone having access to information about the options from which they choose. State and federal governments intervene to protect fairness in the marketplace by implementing antitrust, labor–relations and product–safety laws designed to ensure that free markets remain fair and do not degenerate into a venue for misrepresentation and exploitation. Only if markets are fair and trusted, it's reasoned, can our economy thrive. If there weren't a Food and Drug Administration, would you buy sausage?

The SEC Example

One of the most sweeping marketplace reforms ever undertaken was the establishment of the Security and Exchange Commission after the stock market crash of 1929. Before the SEC, the financial markets were essentially rigged. Manipulators and speculators used them as a means of cornering markets and fleecing the unwary. Insider trading, far from being a crime, was considered normal business practice. The SEC was created to protect investors and the economy and thereby increase both confidence and activity in the markets.

From the 1930's onward, anyone offering securities for sale to the public had to file a registration with the SEC making "full and fair disclosure" of all relevant business and financial information. Public companies are required to disclose the stock holdings, compensation packages, and other interests of their officers and directors. They must file quarterly financial reports that are then made available upon request, and usually at no charge, to anyone who asks for them. All this data is available in a uniform format that makes it possible to inspect and compare one company's performance directly with that of any other company, and to evaluate its financial practices and overall soundness. Similar information is available for limited partnerships and other financial instruments.

The availability of this information does not guarantee that people won't lose money in the stock market, but it does insure that they can see current, comprehensive, and comprehensible information before making their decisions. Sound companies, for their part, make up the expense of this reporting many times over in the increased worth of their operations that results from investor confidence. These reforms, and others that followed from them, are in large part responsible for giving the United States the largest, most orderly, and most secure financial markets in the world. Sunlight, as they say, is the best disinfectant.

Schools Are Not Stocks

We use the financial markets as a point of reference here not because we believe in for–profit schools or because we think that education has much in common with corporate finance, but because the financial markets are the purest form of large–scale dispersed information exchange that we have. Although traders count dollars at the end of the day, what they actually trade in is data. If parents, teachers, administrators, and policy–makers had access to even a fraction of the equivalent information about their own universe, then we might not spend as much time as we do reinventing square wheels for education.

One of the things the government does well is collect information. In the case of the Securities and Exchange Commission, the amount spent in this role is minuscule compared to the hundreds of billions of dollars generated by activities its work makes possible, a fair chunk of which is returned to the government in tax revenue. A similar apparatus designed to serve schools in their activities would, we believe, yield benefits of a different nature, but on a similar scale. In the financial markets, success is measured in its participants' profits. The success of a similar effort centered on schools and learning would be measured in the ongoing, additive improvement to the state of American education.

Mr. Ed

The colleges are in a position to demand openness from curriculum developers and testing companies. As we mentioned, they should only accept courses and tests for which data is available to researchers. However, there's some potential for mischief as institutions start throwing around misleading statistics, and playing many of the games they play now (excluding weak students, for example, to make averages look higher).

Under our plan, the mission of the Department of Education with regard to educational quality would change. Rather than trying to impose a federally sanctioned test (like the National Assessment of Educational Progress, or the ill–conceived American Achievement Tests), the department would emphasize its role as a "secure education commission." The logical place for this effort would be within the existing Office of Educational Research and Improvement. The other functions of the Department of Education, specifically the administration of federal-aid programs to schools and oversight of equity programs, would be unaffected by this.

In this capacity, the Department of Education would have two goals: the enforcement of policies designed to keep the education "markets" fair, and the aggregation and dissemination of information in a standardized, coherent form, a kind of *Consumer Reports* for education. For the latter, it would be responsible for the maintenance of several databases, which would be available for state, local, and private researchers.

The Educational Impact Statement

The first of these would constitute a repository of every curriculum prospectus, or "Educational Impact Statement" (EIS). Under our plan, these would exist as a matter of course—they're a standardized version of the proposals developers would make to colleges, states, and schools for acceptance of their curricula, and what parents and students would review before deciding on a course of study. An EIS would begin with a description of what the curriculum intended to teach, why this was thought important, and how it intended to achieve its goals. Although a curriculum cannot require that a particular textbook or other materials be used, the EIS could and should define in detail what constitutes good in-

> *Remember that the original mandate of the Department of Education was "collecting such statistics and facts as shall show the condition and progress of education in the several States and Territories, and of diffusing such information respecting the organization and management of schools and school systems, and methods of teaching, as shall aid the people of the United States in the establishment and maintenance of efficient school systems."*

structional material for that course of study. The EIS would also describe the curriculum's evaluation philosophy and provide a copy of a sample test.

The government wouldn't be adding much here—its role would *not* be to evaluate or in any way pass judgment on the contents of the EIS, but only to ensure it is presented in a standardized form, and to provide for its wide and efficient dissemination through such means as the Internet and local libraries.

School Directory

A second database would contain information about individual schools. Are they urban, suburban, or rural? In what kind of shape is the building? What's the average amount of money spent per student on teachers and books? What percentage of the staff is actually teaching? What's the administrative overhead?

This database would also contain data about each course offered by the school: Does it tie into one of the Multiple National Curricula? How many sessions are there in a school year? How long are they? What textbooks or other materials are students given? What tests do they take? Are the tests given as the final exam? In what grade are the students? What's the class size? Who is the teacher?

Any state, of course, would be free to require more information of its schools than did the Department of Education. States might want to include things like number of dollars spent on special education, the size of the library, administrative costs, student/computer ratios, or dollars per child spent on sports programs. Schools themselves might want to provide additional information that would help parents and students get a better picture, and there could be space set aside for the school to explain its mission, philosophy, or history.

Student Directory

The third and related database consists of information about students. It keeps track of the students' sex, age, family income, zip code, classes, teachers, grades, and other important educational and demographic information, and it does so under protocols that are both blinded and anonymous, so that no information can ever be traced back to a particular individual.

This information is required if we want to be able to determine the value added by particular teachers and schools, the effect of administrative policies like the length of class periods or the number of days in a school year, the impact of legislative mandates on spending or teacher training, or demographic factors like race, family income, the impact of population density, and availability of health care.

We understand there are privacy issues here (we'll address them in a little while), but such information needs to be gathered. Together with the test-response data maintained by curriculum developers, it would enable researchers, educators, test developers, and anyone else who's interested to analyze the performance of different groups on a particular curriculum. It took years to establish the SAT's bias against women because ETS controlled the demographic and test-response information. Under our proposal, the light shines through for anyone who cares to look.

> The creation of a database of this ilk is already under consideration by the National Education Goals Panel. With a zeal we wouldn't try to match, the panel would keep information like birth weight, number of years in a preschool program, number of moves in the last five years, and extracurricular activities. To learn more, ask the National Education Goals Panel for Publication 93-03.

Making the Data Available

These three federal databases would be available to all interested parties, for the incremental cost of providing the data itself. The Department of Education would also mandate that the curriculum developers make test data available to researchers on the same cost–only terms. This would consist of not only the scores for each student, but the raw data beneath it—the answers to each question for each student who took the test (obviously, some types of tests would be difficult to store this way—we'll take whatever's in there). This information would tie back to the student database maintained by the government, but be similarly blinded so that it could not be associated with any particular student.

For families and others who needed information on only a few dozen schools, the expense of providing this info would be so small that it would not be worth charging for. For researchers, publishers, and entrepreneurs who needed information on thousands or tens of thousands of schools, the cost might run to a few thousand dollars. That might sound expensive, but it's a trivial amount for the people who would ask for it, and is much less than it would cost to acquire such information today, if indeed it were possible to obtain at all.

We would expect that the people who requested this data would be the same sort of people who request most data from the government: researchers, watchdog groups, and people trying to make money from it. The first two would be looking for evidence relating to issues of school funding, educational priorities, and pedagogical or organizational effectiveness.

Ironically, it's the third group, the entrepreneurs who, through aggressive marketing of products designed to help parents and educators make good choices about what goes on in schools, would probably have the most immediate impact on the quality of American education. Just ten years ago, only large institutions could handle the gigabytes of raw data that would be generated in the course of implementing the Multiple National Curriculum proposal. Today, though, a computer capable of processing this information costs less than $5,000, and can be found in almost every office, many homes, and even a few schools throughout the United States.

Educational Information Industry

The public and private sectors have complementary roles in providing us with information. Most of us don't want the government telling us what to eat, or what to drive, or what Spanish course we should take; we want the facts so we can make our own decisions. At the same time, with so much raw information floating around, we're willing to pay people to process it for us.

In the financial markets mutual fund guidebooks, investment letters, software packages, and on–line services massage raw data into optimally useful form. Relatively little of the information on which these products are based is proprietary: you could get it for free from a library or from the SEC. Yet millions of people feel it's worth some expense to have the basic data digested into a more accessible and comprehensible format.

The new education data produced by the plan would encourage the creation of a new industry similar to that which has grown up around financial products and services. Since the raw data would be overwhelming to most people, interpretation will become very important. Articles, books, videos, computer programs, and seminars would help parents and schools acquire and evaluate the data they needed.

As in the case of public companies, most schools would quickly come to see the prospectus as an opportunity rather than a burden. People increasingly base their choices of products and services on the quality of information they receive about them. Schools, as individual orga-

This would generate a classic "free rider" effect, whereby those who cannot afford these products benefit from the expenditures of those who can. The public scrutiny and subsequent debate will affect all parents in all schools, regardless of whether or not they purchase guide books.

nizations and as a collective social institution, should not stand apart from this trend. The openness schools project, the sense of working in partnership with their families, can be the first step in the necessary adventure of making parents, colleges, and the business community into allies and partners as well as clients. It will be good business and good policy to take advantage of this opportunity. Schools unable to flourish in such a climate of openness and accountability would, and should, wither away.

Data Privacy

Americans currently have less data privacy and less control over personal information like health care and transaction records than any people in the industrialized world.[1]

The subject of data privacy in a digital age is far too important and wide-ranging for us to do justice to here. Any endeavor to collect information about people, especially over long periods of time and on a broad scale, needs to take privacy and data security very seriously right from the start. The Multiple National Curricula plan would create several huge databases containing information about millions of individuals and institutions. While this is relatively straightforward from a technical point of view, the creation of such a database poses social and ethical questions which cannot be ignored.[2]

The greatest danger is not from digital vandals or cloak–and–dagger system crackers (although these are worth attending to), but from fully authorized and sanctioned persons or agencies using the data in ways that were not originally intended or of which people are not aware. The ease with which multiple databases can be cross–linked is what makes it possible for direct marketers to compare your credit-card purchases with, say, your car registration or house title (available from your state, in most cases) to decide whether you would be a likely candidate for a telemarketing pitch on Hawaiian condominiums. The Internal Revenue Service does the same thing to check the records of your purchases against your reported income to help decide whether your tax returns are on the level.

The Multiple National Curricula plan will yield the greatest benefits if we can reference, say, a student's ninth-grade social-studies grade and test scores to the textbooks she used and her parents' income. Or if we can track the performance of a teacher across several years in different settings to determine with which type of kids and in what kind of curricular environment he performs best, correlating this with such things as his educational background and age. Yet we have no right to ask for all this information—let alone to store it—unless we can guarantee that it will be used only for the purposes for which it was originally collected.

Fortunately, the technology exists to permit the collection of detailed records that follow individual performance across time, without linking them to an identifiable real–world person. Theoretical and practical advances in cryptography, anonymized record keeping, and digital authentication permit record–keeping that is detailed, appropriate, and secure. The same computerized technologies that support policies which undermine privacy can be used to support policies which enhance it, provided we make the effort to ensure that they do.

These data protection concerns are crucial, and it may well be decided that it's not worth jeopardizing students' privacy to improve our educational system in this way. If these issues can't be resolved, though, we could decide to not collect certain categories of information and get a lot out of the plan anyway.

The Prospectus

Because of the ease with which large–scale aggregate numbers like these can be manipulated or misinterpreted, it's important that certain other information be made available from every school in order to make the numbers truthful and meaningful. For example, an unscrupulous school could make itself look stronger than it really is by encouraging weak students to skip their end–of–year assessments. If we're not careful, we will see data thrown together in misleading or fraudulent ways intended to "prove" that some school, teacher, state, or textbook is better or worse than its competition. There are many ways to present data, and some have been established as being inherently less misleading than others. Therefore it's important that we choose the ground rules before starting the game.

Once again, the financial markets can provide some guidance. The Securities and Exchange Commission not only dictates the

For years, Secretaries of Education have published the average SAT scores of each state. Every year, they praised the states at the top of the list for their great work, and noted that scores didn't correlate with per–pupil spending. What was their secret? Simple: in those high–scoring states, only 3 percent of the students took the SAT. Which 3 percent? The highest achieving kids, of course, those who were applying to prestigious out–of–state colleges. States with the lowest scores had the greatest percentage of kids taking the SAT, as high as 60 percent of all students, so many more average and mediocre students were included in the sample. Comparisons of two such divergent populations were utterly meaningless, but you didn't find that out in USA Today, or on network news for that matter.

substance of what companies must disclose, it also requires that the data be presented uniformly, according to Generally Accepted Accounting Principles. For example, every company listed on the stock market handles depreciation of a factory building in similar ways, or explains why it does not. Under our proposal, the Department of Education would have the additional responsibility of setting the principles for proper disclosure of information and monitoring the industry to make sure that everyone is holding to them. Since you don't want to give schools an incentive to discourage achievement, for instance, Generally Accepted Reporting Procedures would establish that a school's reported scores should reflect both the number of students and the percentage of the class that took a test, as well as those students' performance.

While each school should be able to promote, advertise, or represent itself in any legal way it wishes, certain standardized information should accompany any promotional materials, as is the case with financial products directed at general investors. As part of the school registration process each year, parents and students would participate in an educative "informed consent" process to help them interpret the school and curricula prospectuses. This process would also ensure that parents were aware of the student body's performance on tests attached to the school's chosen curricula. Parents could not then claim, nor could school administrators hide behind, a general ignorance of the conditions at their school.

The reporting of this information would impose little hardship on schools, since they already collect most of it for reporting to state and federal agencies. The school prospectus would simply ensure that the data is presented in a standard format and widely disseminated to the public. The Department of Education would, either at random intervals or upon suspicion of misrepresentation, conduct audits to ensure that the information supplied by schools is accurate and complete. Should fraud or misrepresentation be discovered, it would indicate that finding in the school's prospectus, say for the next five years, and conduct yearly audits of school data until it is error free for some period of time. The threat

A school prospectus should contain whatever parents find most valuable in helping them to choose and assess their children's education. It might include: percentage of ninth graders who graduate from the school, percentage of graduates who go on to two- or four-year colleges, school crime rate, and the number of teachers with advanced degrees in their fields. All citizens, not just those with school-age children, have an obligation to be informed about the conditions in their schools. The prospectus should include a glossary of important terms and concepts, and state and national averages for important figures. In order to avoid a simplistic "shop-by-numbers" mentality, it would include boilerplate explanations of where and why comparisons with state and national averages might be misleading.

of such a banner in their prospectus, the academic equivalent of a scarlet letter would be a forceful enough deterrent that the Department of Education would need no new legal enforcement powers.

No Red Tape

In fulfilling its new functions, the Department of Education would be unlike the state and federal education agencies with which we are currently familiar. It would not advocate a particular form of schooling or exercise any authority over what goes on in classrooms. It would not approve or reject any curriculum. It would not require any changes to any curriculum. And it would not advocate that the states adopt any curriculum.

This plan doesn't call for any new layers of management. It would not be a source of empty rhetoric or dead–end initiatives. It would simply make certain that every parent has access to relevant, up–to–date information about the schools in his or her community.

This relatively simple and inexpensive innovation would yield tremendous benefits almost immediately. Students and parents would have an accurate picture of their schools' strengths and weaknesses. Teachers and administrators would have a more informed, involved, and responsible clientele with which to work. School boards and state agencies, should they continue to exist, would have easily accessible data to assist them in their quality–control missions. The federal government would be playing a tangible, constructive role in helping states implement their own goals for their own schools. And the entire data–collection mechanism would cost a minuscule fraction of the $250 billion of public money that is spent on K–12 education each year.

And It Pays for Itself!

If you're concerned about the cost of this database, it's simple enough to charge a small royalty on any guidebooks, magazines, or other productions that use this data. Part of this revenue stream could be used by the Department of Education to pay for the cost of record-keeping. The rest could fund state and federal efforts that help disadvantaged families and communities make the best use of this information. This proves especially important because most reforms that have, like this one, focused on giving people power to speak up, exert pressure, and make choices have tended to most benefit those who are already

> At the risk of repeating ourselves. The national curricula that we're proposing would be created by independent organizations. The main role of the federal government would be information collection and dissemination.

> We now have enough experience with public-school choice programs to know that we need to be cautious when making assumptions about how people will act when given information with which to make choices about education. Seeking out and making use of statistical information is a middle–class pastime, and the people in this country who most need their schools to improve are not middle–class. One of the goals of our plan is to encourage people from all backgrounds to participate actively in securing quality education for their kids. Those who have been traditionally disadvantaged by their own past education will need assistance in learning how to successfully navigate this terrain.

most privileged.

Since the actual collection of data is even now a mostly routine part of school operation, the largest part of the costs incurred by the government would be for the publication of the school prospectuses; ideally, every family would automatically receive a copy of the report for their school, in their home language, at the time the reports are issued. Both school districts and individual schools would probably want to hold meetings for their parents, students, and staff to answer questions and outline goals, trends, and policies not fully explained in the reports.

Keeping it Fair

The Department of Education would have one other role, also a traditional government responsibility: discouraging anticompetitive behavior.

For over a hundred years a tremendous amount of money has been spent on public education. It has long been a market in every sense of the word (albeit a severely distorted one), but with little oversight or intervention to ensure its fairness and efficiency. Especially during the shift to a more decentralized model, the government should keep its eyes open. To create fair markets, for instance, we should keep colleges out of the admissions-testing business, and should keep testing companies out of the textbook and preparation business.

For example, suppose Harvard decided to create a curriculum and assessment for, say, English literature. While it couldn't require students to take this course over another, parents would rightly wonder whether Harvard would look more favorably on those students who took its test. This built–in advantage would work strongly against the success of other curricula and give the colleges too much power to limit their number.

Or suppose a group of colleges joined together to sponsor a test. To the degree they benefited financially from one test, there would be no incentive for them to accept any others; a potential applicant would have to take *their* test, and pay *their* test fee.

The resulting lack of competition would smother innovation. We've seen this before: The SAT is sponsored by the College Board (made up of the colleges themselves). In the last fifty years, it has been changed twice, both times superficially. Think about how much cars, computers, television, telephones, and everything else has evolved in fifty years. But why bother changing the test if everyone has to take it anyway?

It would also be wrong for the test developers to sell textbooks and prep materials for their own tests. The conflicts of interest would be enormous ("SAT preparation from the people who make up the test" boasts a recent College Board flyer), and the anticompetitive effects obvious: How can fair competition between textbooks exist when one player already knows the answers?

In Japan, each selective college has its own admissions test. Students from all over the country spend a week in Tokyo, taking one test after another. While this results in a higher standard that any government-mandated tests, it adds to the tremendous pressure that students there face. It would also be highly impractical in a country as large as this one.

Perhaps we're being overly protective of the free market here. It's possible that the Ivy League schools could jointly sponsor a test but still accept others. And it's possible that schools would shun the testing companies texts for those of third parties. But why create a market and then rig it? Let's start by keeping everyone separate, and only break down these walls if there's some compelling reason to do so.

Knowledge is Good

In looking to the Department of Education to monitor this new system, we're betting that the government is better at collecting data and policing markets than it is at running things. While it's possible that the colleges could craft the rules of the game so well that government intervention will be unnecessary, the maintenance of proper databases and the enforcement of antitrust rules will certainly make this plan even more effective.

Especially the data. You can't manage what you can't measure. You can't make good judgments or fair comparisons unless you have good information on which to base them. And as we're about to see, Multiple National Curricula could revolutionize American education once we have that information.

CHAPTER 8

The World After

You Can't Hit What You Can't See

We have now created a mechanism for gathering a tremendous amount of information and a means to put it to work. That in itself is nothing special: Educational data, especially testing data, has been available for a long time although never on the scale or of the quality we anticipate. In the past it was created by and for administrators, mostly as a means of centralizing control. The first standardized test was given by reformers in Boston in 1844. Their goal was to demonstrate empirically that schools throughout the city were too variable in quality and should therefore be governed by a central board. By the 1930s, most states had instituted performance testing programs.

Those who established these programs never imagined, however, that the information would or should be used as a means of holding schools up to public scrutiny. Even today, most teachers and administrators are uncomfortable with the idea of putting detailed information into the hands of those who might hold schools accountable from "outside" the system.

Such resistance is not entirely without merit. First of all, *you* might be uncomfortable if strangers were publicly evaluating your job performance. Ratings and ranking by themselves are worse than meaningless: They're full of hidden assumptions that may or may not reflect the realities of the situation they seek to capture. The point of the Multiple National Curricula plan is not to burden schools further with simple-minded rankings masquerading as benchmarks. Furthermore, even good information doesn't mean very much without some means to act on it. What those means are and who gets to use them are as important to defining the character of a system as the source and quality of the information itself. We've seen that the history of public schooling has been in part an ongoing struggle between professionals and lay people, between administrators and workers, and between local and distant centers of gravity. Information and the means to use it are necessarily tools of power in this struggle. The Multiple National Curricula plan attempts to make information broadly and deeply available to anyone with an interest in it. That is one of the fundamental differences between it and everything that has come before.

A Textbook Market That Works

Few institutions are as recalcitrant as public education. The interests that make it up, competitive as they may be among themselves, have managed over time to forge a remarkably resilient structure that seems to resist nearly all forces for change. One chink in the armor, we believe, is the textbook companies. Despite their tremendous influence in shaping curricula, they must nevertheless respond to market forces and deliver the product that is asked for. Unlike teachers, they lack the moral and political authority to lobby public opinion against plans that upset their applecart and, at any rate, big change is good for their bottom line since it usually means the production and purchase of new materials. The Multiple National Curricula plan harnesses this self–interest to improve learning.

For example, let's assume that there will be several different textbooks available for use by teachers who work with the Pfizer biology curriculum and its accompanying exam. Since the data will exist, someone (perhaps the publishers themselves) will correlate performance on the test with the different textbooks used by the schools (adjusted against the demographics of the schools), and determine which textbook best helped prepare students for the exam.

Many magazines and newspapers regularly feature stories that evaluate colleges, graduate schools, and professional schools. Imagine a magazine article came out showing that the Random House or the MTV textbook for the Pfizer biology course was the best by a wide margin. If you were a biology teacher (using that curriculum) or a principal with a choice, would you continue to recommend your old text? If you were a state administrator, wouldn't you want your schools and teachers to be able to make use of the best and most up–to–date materials? If you were another textbook company, wouldn't you change your textbook to better suit the curriculum and the test? And if you were Random House or MTV, would you rest on your laurels, or would you continue to hone your product to stay in front of your competition?

> *Textbook companies compete now, but they're working in relative obscurity to please a handful of state adoption committees. Breaking down the market into much smaller segments will encourage smaller publishing houses to compete. And now the competition will be over actual performance, not nice bindings.*

This kind of continual scrutiny—and the market pressure towards innovation that comes with it—will change the way textbook companies think about their products. As we've discussed, they will already be replacing their massive tomes with materials focused closely on specific programs of study. Multiple National Curricula encourage the formation of dozens or even hundreds of new approaches to learning, each representing a potentially profitable micromarket in which instructional materials vendors will compete vigorously by offering better and better products. The more marginal or underserved a group, an idea, or an approach is today, the more it will benefit from this new alignment.

Nextbooks

But the plan is about more than just refining the materials that exist today. Many of the current problems with textbooks derive from their use as a support for inadequate models of teaching. Textbooks, like teachers, are expected to contain everything students will need to know about a particular subject. Using chapter divisions, homework questions, and canned exams, they are expected to impose a predefined structure on their subject area as well as on students' patterns of work. This approach was in harmony with nineteenth century factory models of education. But as models of education change and teachers become more like guides and less like authoritarian sages, textbooks will change, too.

With more and more schools connecting to networks (the figure now is around 10 percent and growing rapidly), and more and more educational resources taking nontraditional forms (museum programs, internships, interactive CD–ROM, mentor programs), textbooks in many fields will metamorphose at least partially from a collection of facts and figures into a compilation of pointers to reach resource bases—tables of contents for what's available beyond the physical walls of the schools or the mind of the teacher. The term "textbooks" will no longer adequately characterize their role in education.

When producing materials for this kind of environment, corporate size is not the competitive advantage it is now. Having the motivation to stay on top of new developments in educational resources, the flexibility to work within innovative cross–disciplinary collaborations, the responsiveness to collect and present information in ways that help kids and teachers make a new kind of sense, will be far more valuable under our plan than having the throw weight to cajole, bribe, and bully textbook adoption committees.

Of course, large publishers will still have strong assets in their existing infrastructure of researchers, artists, consultants, and contacts with school agencies. They will retain economies of scale in the actual production of books, and can accept contracts to produce instructional materials designed by others. Most large publishers are already experimenting with, collaborating on, or deploying mechanisms for electronic delivery of multimedia "texts." Within the Multiple National Curricula system, however, they will have to compete on the basis of quality with hundreds of small cooperative ventures established for the sole purpose of producing materials for one curriculum, one school district, or one state. To succeed in this radically decentralized environment, they will have to engage in ongoing collaboration with those who design and teach the multiple curricula.

Multiple National Curricula will go far toward leveling the instructional materials playing field. It will provide testing grounds for small or nontraditional publishers of instructional materials. With just a few thousand students around the country, they will be able to prove the quality of those materials. And once teachers can compare the scores of students who follow a common curriculum but use different texts, the folks with the best materials will be tough to beat.

Helping Your Kids

There are three major obstacles for parents today who want to help their kids to thrive academically. First, they usually have little advance idea what their children are supposed to be learning. Second, they have few standards against which to judge how well their children have learned what's been taught, other than the teacher's own exams. Third, they have little voice in deciding what's taught.

The advantages of the Multiple National Curricula model are clear. First, the Educational Impact Statement will provide a road map of the material that will be covered each semester and the relative importance of each part of the course. Second, published benchmarks will allow parents to judge the student's performance against other students covering the same material. Third, the curriculum selection process encourages parents and teachers to become involved in choosing which of the many available curricula will be taught at their school.

Few Tools

As important as it is for parents to know what their kids are learning in school, it's just as important to give them the tools to do something about it. Right now, the ancillary market in American education is largely limited to remedial tutoring since, although you don't know what your child will be learning this year, you do have *some* idea what he was supposed to have learned the year before. Predictably, there is also a huge market surrounding the SAT, the one target at which everyone can aim. There are literally thousands of tutors, scores of books, dozens of courses, and assorted videos and computer programs willing to help you prepare for this test.

Many students don't need any help to excel in school. But access to a range of appropriate tools would be one of the biggest benefits of Multiple National Curricula. Imagine that your son was having trouble conjugating verbs in Spanish, or understanding orbitals in chemistry. Catalogues of software, videos, books, and courses would be available to help him, along with any number of articles rating and discussing the change in performance attributable to each one.

Some of these tools are available now for academic subjects. There are, for example, excellent math books and software on the market. However, since they're not linked to a particular curriculum, they each teach math from scratch, not knowing how much you've already seen or mastered, or where a particular concept fits into your larger course of study. There's no way to know which is most helpful, and which will actually hurt your performance by using an approach completely different from your teacher's.

New Tools

What services would become available if everyone knew what the high school was trying to teach a student this year in history class? First, books that focused on some of the most important periods in the course, perhaps providing first-person accounts, comments from scholars of the era, and comparisons between some of the issues of that time and those facing the student. Conceivably, this printed material might not come out in book form, but as periodicals ("Subscribe to *American History Review!*"). As multimedia tools evolve, they would begin to appear for both home and library use. In content, they would be sophisticated versions of the textbooks, able to adapt themselves to a student's areas of strength and weakness, while bringing the material to life through sound and video. These might appear as stand-alone CD–ROMs, or be made available over computer networks or cable television.

Since the reputations of schools and teachers will benefit from higher scores on the national assessments (just as they do now from high SAT or AP scores), we could expect that some of these "ancillary" tools would be bought by the school for their students. Since the assessment at which this enrichment is directed is closely tied to the curriculum and covers it in meaningful detail, test prep will serve to strengthen the curriculum, rather than compete with it as SAT prep does now.

Under the Multiple National Curriculum plan, the para–educational market would help increase a school's impact. And unlike what currently exists, the new tools would not focus exclusively on the needs of middle–class and wealthy students. Teachers, administrators, and researchers would pore over the data to discover which tools worked best with which demographic groups, opening new niches for smaller companies to fill, and bringing more support services to the disadvantaged. Some of these programs might be funded with public money, as is currently the case with programs targeted at poor kids and special-education students. Some will be financed privately, through foundations working in conjunction with schools of education. Perhaps the most significant contributions will be those developed by networks of teachers and support service personnel who work with these kids day in and day out.

Schools may teach the scientific method, but few of them use it. There is no rigorous record keeping when a teacher tries a new way of teaching a subject, and no real way to judge if the new approach was more or less effective than the old. A single national curriculum would allow the proper evaluation of new approaches. But such experimentation would be limited to finding out what best conveys the lowest-common-denominator questions from the single national exam, and be severely restrained by the need to adhere to the guidelines of that single curriculum. Under our proposal thousands of experiments would be going on every year, as teachers tried to discover the best way to teach umpteen different bodies of material.

Appraising Your School

With the information available under our plan it will be possible to make comparisons among similar schools that use the same curricula. Schools in turn will be able to see what value an individual teacher adds. They'll do this by evaluating his students' performance not against abstract goals or arbitrary assessment criteria but against the actual performance of similar students around the country who are learning the same things.

Suppose that kids in Norman, Oklahoma are achieving the nationwide average of 415 in the Stanford calculus curriculum while kids in the nearby town of Moore are running around 322 in the same course. Both communities would be interested in knowing what it is that the schools in Norman are doing better. Do they have fewer kids in their classes? A hot breakfast program? More hours of homework? Multimedia technology? Better textbooks? Or are their teachers just doing a better job?

As a Moore parent, you would certainly want to know why students in your school were not doing well on the same calculus course that kids in nearby schools were acing. The school administration might not want you to know, but that really shouldn't be their decision: they're *your* kids. Conversely, if your kids were doing better than those in other schools, and it was pretty clear that it was attributable to smaller class sizes or more highly paid teachers, then you might want to think twice before supporting that initiative to cut back on school funding.

The Multiple National Curricula plan is designed to give you information you can use to exercise influence over decisions made about the education of the children in your community. Chances are good, therefore, that your school board, school administration, teachers' union, and state Office of Education will resist it, because it is the first step towards a system of real accountability that shifts the center of evaluation back towards the parents.

Keeping Score

But opponents of the plan won't say that. They'll say that using numbers to compare schools invites superficial comparisons, that test scores fail to capture all the richness of the educative experience, that it is unfair to hold schools and teachers responsible for complex outcomes like drop–out rates. They'll say that such information will cause students to flee already embattled public schools and accelerate the decline of common schooling. These inevitable criticisms will be correct on the details, but wrong on the big picture.

Having more—and more accurate—information on which to base a judgment is never a bad thing. Are academic success rates or percentage of expenditures devoted to administrative overhead less adequate or more misleading indicators of school quality than the football team's win–loss record or where the French club goes for spring break? Does the percentage of parents who perform volunteer work at the school fully capture the experience of being a student at that school? Of course not, but this and other information are places to begin a more thorough investigation. Is it desirable or even possible to compare schools against one another on the basis of their relative performance on various national tests? Sure, if it's kept in perspective.

America likes to rank things. We rank test scores. We rank standards of living. We rank television audiences. We rank our Representatives. We rank appliances. We rank things that can't even be measured, like "most livable city," "best company to work for," or "best undergraduate education." We care more about *which* thing is "best" than *why* it is.

And yet people buy toasters that Consumer Reports doesn't like, and people live in even the "least livable" cities. School prospectuses are not only about rankings. The point is not only to discover which schools have the most or least success, but *why* they do. The numbers in the prospectus represent a point of departure, a basis for inquiry, a doorway rather than a billboard. Schools will and should have to put them into context. The information in the prospectus—good, bad, or indifferent—is the school's mandate for establishing an ongoing dialogue with its communities and its customers. Schools and teachers will undoubtedly be compared with others teaching similar sets of curricula. But if history is any guide, these numbers will be one of many criteria used to judge them.

Sure, there will be newspaper headlines about "the worst school in the country" and parent demands for the execution of everyone teaching in poorly performing departments. Those things happen now; they're just not based on anything. But there will also be discussion between schools and parents about the connections between inputs like class size, teacher experience, and administrative overhead, and outputs like test scores, graduation rates, and success on the job or in college.

Remember—the whole point of the proposal was to get to this place. The act of shining a light on something often causes it to improve. Where this is not enough, the Multiple National Curricula plan makes it easier for district or state quality assurance teams to focus resources where they're most needed and can do the most good. Before torching weaker schools and teachers (we'll discuss school choice in chapter ten), this system will give them the opportunity to improve.

Schools will be competing not just with other schools but with their own past performance. With useful data on tap, parents will come to expect year–over–year improvements rather than schools that tread water. In most normal environments, people try to do a good job. It's a measure of how strongly schools have disfranchised and demotivated their teachers and administrators that the chance to perform could be widely viewed as a threat.

Feedback Loop

In the past, school rankings and other official reports were the end of a process, something that happened *to* schools. Here, they would be part of a process that schools themselves would drive. Since schools, teachers, and parents would be in active collaboration with curriculum designers (and, one step removed, universities), the natural tendency will be for information to flow through the system, information on what works, what works better, and what doesn't work at all. Even today, schools that are successful would generally be happy to share the reasons for their success, if they knew what they were and if they had a mechanism for spreading the word.

Many of today's school improvement efforts—the Coalition for Essential Schools, Apple's Classrooms of Tomorrow, the Department of Education's Education Programs That Work—are basically networks to monitor and disseminate classroom- and school-level data. This is the type of information we hope to make widely, cheaply, and usefully available to every school.

At the other end of the spectrum, weaker schools would generally love to do a better job. Just as a good company can motivate its people without the constant threat of firing them, we believe that most educators can be motivated without the pressure of the school–choice marketplace or the threat of state takeovers.

Of course, sometimes more benign motivators are not enough (even the best companies have to fire people). In some schools, the tools that could improve things will lie unused in a file cabinet. It's also possible that many citizens won't make use of statistical information to encourage change (after all, parents of kids in bad schools have always known how bad their schools are and haven't been able to do much about it).

But this plan isn't about giving schools or parents a couple of new numbers to boast or to complain about. It's about creating marketplaces of curricula, textbooks, schools, and teachers. There is competition in the car or computer markets not because the manufacturers know the relative performance of their products, but because their customers do.

The Multiple National Curricula plan allows meaningful, officially certified comparison at the school and classroom level. It allows practitioners and administrators to better isolate relevant causes and effects. It lays the foundation for a support network among those using the same curricula that includes fellow teachers, instructional designers, and university–based specialists. Most importantly, the standardization and rigor that accompany the assessment process legitimizes diversity and flexibility in teaching and administration. This gives teachers and schools the freedom to try new things when the old ones aren't working—a freedom they mostly lack now—and it makes communities and state administrators accountable to each school for the support they do or don't provide it as another variable in a multivariate analysis. It allows schools, for the first time, to demand more than just money and lip service.

Superstar Teachers

America celebrates those whose performance it can quantify: the highest scorers in the NBA, the CEOs of the largest companies, the best-selling authors. When we can confidently say, "That woman is among the best English teachers in the country," she will be celebrated as well. With that celebration will come the perks—money and career options—with which we reward other talented professionals.

We already have numerous Teacher of the Year awards. Most people (including teachers) recognize them for the meaningless "gold stars" that they are. By making it possible to determine the value added by individual instructors, Multiple National Curricula encourage the development of a genuine star system for teachers.

If you're the principal or PTA head of a school whose English department is routinely in the top tier of schools using its curriculum, you would be most unhappy to lose those teachers. If you're the principal of a neighboring school, it might occur to you to attempt to recruit them by offering a better salary. As the head of a textbook company, you might pay those teachers to endorse your text (or to edit it). A company that runs seminars for English teachers would certainly want them on staff. As crass as it sounds, we'll know that the phrase "best English teacher" means something when it starts to be worth money.

Throwing Money Around

Some teachers and union representatives will probably claim that such a star system is undignified, that teachers do what they do for love and love alone. Nonsense. Our society believes in rewarding performance. For better or for worse, we tend to respect those whom we reward more than those we do not. Kids certainly know this. They contrast the poorly remunerated obscurity in which most teachers work with the wealth and attention that surrounds stars of all sorts, and rightly conclude that this society does not value teaching or learning very highly.

No amount of pious exhortation from elected officials will change that perception as long as it is fundamentally correct. To paraphrase Jim Wright of Texas when he fought against the school funding cutbacks of the 1980s, throwing money at problems may not solve them, but throwing words at them certainly won't.

But it's not enough to simply pay teachers more. Higher teacher pay doesn't correlate with increased student achievement because across–the–board increases go to good and bad teachers alike. If money is to be an effective incentive it has to be tied to some index of performance. It's difficult to think of any job, let alone any profession, where there is no benchmark against which to measure an individual's productivity, where measurable accomplishments simply do not exist. The Multiple National Curricula plan offers a base upon which to build an appropriate system of performance–based rewards and sanctions.

What Works

But pay raises may be the least important thing about the teacher statistics generated by our plan. As the numbers come in, teachers will gain a lot of feedback about what works best for them. Are they most effective with older or younger students? Stronger or weaker ones? Boys or girls? Which curriculum does their style best fit? Good teachers, like anyone else, will seek to build on strengths and address or avoid areas of weakness.

It is worth remembering that real progress in teaching, as in most other crafts, comes from the steady, workaday development in craft and knowledge that is gained from the commonplace experience of thousands of practitioners. While our plan supports and encourages stars—every worthwhile endeavor needs exemplars—Multiple National Curricula also recognizes that the mainstay of children's education is the teacher in their classroom, and it supports that teacher by providing her with the benefits of the ongoing, continually refined and tested experience of her peers.

Curricula Evolve, Too

Most school–improvement discussion centers on implementation. It's teachers and schools that need to change, the thinking goes, not what they teach. If kids aren't learning chemistry or math, the problem must be the teacher, the student, or the school. With the exception of the rare cataclysm like "New Math" in the 1960's, the body of knowledge that is held to be appropriate for transmission in schools remains pretty much unscrutinized.

The kind of attention that focuses solely on teaching performance, practice, and assessment—open classrooms, outcome–based education, portfolio assessment, and the like—without considering content at all is one–dimensional. It over-emphasizes method and either ignores the question of what content is most educationally effective, or allows the method (either of teaching or of assessment) to determine the content of what's taught. Such approaches are fragmentary. They lack the vision and the tools to examine the ways in which the interplay of content, pedagogy, and assessment determine educational outcomes.

The Multiple National Curricula plan provides the vision *and* the tools. After just a few years, it will provide sufficiently rich longitudinal data to determine how the various curricula affect later outcomes, whether in college, on the job, or in the wider world. It will be possible, for instance, to inquire whether the inclusion of more poetry instruction correlates with stronger writing skills or a greater percentage of English majors in college; whether the ubiquitous "drug resistance" programs make as much difference as adults believe or as little difference as students believe; whether performing dissections in biology makes for a better grasp of science; whether Afrocentric environments do or do not have a positive impact on the long–term outcomes of African–American students.

This wealth of data will enable curriculum sponsors to fine–tune, expand, or junk entire sections of curricula based on the real–world performance of students and ongoing feedback from teachers, administrators, and offices of education. It will permit curriculum development to become more rationalized, its theories more verifiable, its values and assumptions less covert, its outcomes less haphazard. Teachers (and others who select curricula) will see the impact of their choices on their students' futures.

> As we've been emphasizing throughout this book, many significant factors determine educational outcome, including poverty, access, and cultural values. We're intentionally limiting our discussion to those factors which schools can most directly control.

Colleges will be in an especially strong position to evaluate the real–world effects of high school curricula on higher–order thinking skills. Given that they *started* this reform, they'll have both the interest and the ability to see how performance on those tests correlates with success in their college. Their data will help them reevaluate initial decisions on the acceptability of each curricula and keep them involved in the improvement process, bringing them into closer partnership with teachers and administrators on the high-school level.

Still, colleges will be only one site of curricular development. The Multiple National Curricula plan decentralizes curriculum creation and improvement by extending it out from the universities and state offices of education and distributing the initiative and the responsibility to thousands of potential developers. Unlike many forms of decentralization, our plan does not lessen mechanisms for accountability but rather strengthens them. Throughout the history of the public education, some (mostly teachers and students) have lived in glass houses, subject to continual observation while others (mostly administrators and academics) have lived in fortified bunkers essentially shielded from scrutiny and meaningful accountability. This plan moves everyone in the "education village" into sturdy, adaptable, and publicly accessible accommodations where they can work together towards their common goal.

Do Rising Hemlines Cause Bull Markets?

The Multiple National Curricula plan relies on the accumulation and dissemination of vast quantities of data. This reliance can have serious undesirable consequences if not given some forethought.

The first danger is the repetition of the perpetual social–scientific confusion of correlation with causality. Just because two pieces of data increase or decrease together doesn't mean we can say that those changes are connected in any meaningful way. For instance, college tuitions have risen dramatically during the last fifteen years. Over that same period of time the universe has been expanding (though somewhat more slowly). If you were to plot these two patterns together, you would find near–perfect correlation. Yet it would probably be a mistake to conclude that rising tuitions caused the expansion of the universe, or vice versa.

Not all correlation–causality misinterpretations are this obvious. A recent study reported that poverty was strongly associated with increased risks of heart disease. Some interpreted this to mean that poverty caused heart disease. It's far more likely, however, that poverty is associated with other factors like bad diet, inadequate medical care, and lack of access to health education that are in fact the underlying causes of the increased risk. Being poor would probably not be bad for your heart if those other factors were addressed.

Education has always had more than its share of correlation–causality confusion. Certain kinds of educational inputs, like class size, seat–hours, and per–pupil expenditure are easily and reliably measured, as are outputs like test scores and graduation rates. This easy measurability encourages researchers to search for the one best explanation for performance, a practice borrowed from economics (the "dismal science," and equally prone to fallacy) and known as production–function analysis. The problem, of course, is that education is even less a science than economics. As anyone who has ever been in a classroom will tell you, it is a rich and complex social practice whose most important elements are difficult if not impossible to quantify.

The Multiple National Curricula plan will produce more diverse, more detailed, more useful, and more controlled data on inputs and outputs than was ever possible before. The large numbers of students, schools, and teachers involved will make it possible to hold a great many variables constant and still have a sample broad enough to base valid conclusions on. The standardization of goals and assessment that is central to the plan, while not airtight (which no system of education could or should want to be), is a significant advance over the completely uncontrolled hodgepodge that now frustrates systematic improvement. We will never know precisely what it is that makes some teachers great, but we will know what factors seem to help that greatness emerge more readily than others.

This plan is not about building a data paradise. Numbers are central to it because they provide an excellent analytic tool, a moment of departure, a talking point. Having numbers with more validity is desirable. But statistics are not a magic bullet or a Holy Grail—it's what we do with them that counts. The Multiple National Curricula/school prospectus plan enlists better data in the service of a system of flexibility, responsiveness, and innovation. Unlike nearly all previous efforts to measure educational inputs and outputs, it puts hard information equally into the hands of teachers, parents, policymakers, colleges, and school administrators, not to encourage snap judgments or draw superficial and inappropriate conclusions, but to support the real collaborative work of discussion, analysis, and implementation by everyone concerned.

You Are Here

So colleges and businesses have required students to take curriculum-bound assessments. High schools, testing companies, state agencies, and parent groups have responded by creating various combinations of curricula and tests, and textbook companies and instructional designers have set out teaching tools for this new world. The government has stepped in to make sure the evolving educational marketplace plays fair and to facilitate the flow of information.

Now the data are coming in, and an industry is growing up to make it intelligible to parents and educators. Textbook companies, schools, and policy makers are watching it closely as they revise products and policies. Tools are coming to market to help students excel in their courses, and the best teachers are starting to command six-figure salaries. Curricula are being altered to address not just ideological concerns but pragmatic ones.

In a very short time, several "marketplaces"—of ideas, of curricula, of tests and textbooks—have sprung into existence, bringing a new level of accountability into the education world. All that's left is to shed a few of the remnants of the old system.

SECTION

Measurable Improvement

3

CHAPTER 9

Implications
for
Teachers

Managing the Inputs

The Multiple National Curricula plan represents a tremendous departure from the way we have historically organized authority and responsibility for instruction. It assumes that, given the chance, teachers would transform their present low–status wage labor into a high–status profession.

Such a change is desperately needed. Right now, teaching holds the lowest status of any "profession" in this country. As both a cause and a result of this lack of status, individual schools and teachers have seen their discretion over how to organize teaching and learning transferred to school boards and state agencies. Central state authorities determine what each school must teach, how long class periods must be, and who may be hired to teach, and so forth.

> Until recently, newly hired teachers in the Boston school system were prohibited by law from learning their school or grade assignments until the day before classes began.

The net result is that, although they are commonly referred to as professionals, teachers have few of the responsibilities or rewards professionals take for granted. Financially, the starting salaries for teachers are lower than those for any other field that requires a bachelor's degree, and salaries top out sooner and lower than those of any other profession. The lack of prestige accorded to teachers is reflected in the overcrowded, poorly equipped, and dangerous environment in which many of them work. Their one consolation is that, since pay is determined solely on the basis of seniority and educational credentials, the quality of their work is by and large irrelevant to the progress of their careers.

Attracting Talent

These conditions—poorly paid, closely supervised work in oppressive environments—mean that teaching attracts and retains those who are either intensely dedicated and willing to sacrifice autonomy, prestige, and financial reward, or those who don't have a lot of other options. While there are no doubt many teachers who are dedicated to their students, it is an unfortunate fact that teaching as a profession is not attracting enough innovative, smart, ambitious role models.

> As of 1990, twenty-two of twenty-three states with grade requirements for teaching certificates set them at about the C+ level (2.5 on a 4.0 scale); those with minimum SAT requirements averaged about 840. By way of comparison, the NCAA requires that college athletes with a C average score at least 900 on the SAT in order to attain eligibility (and plans to toughen those requirements next year).

Aimee and Craig Howley and Edwina Pendarvis have collected a number of studies concerning teacher characteristics.[1] They demonstrate that high-school seniors and college students who intend to major in education have lower academic aptitude than those who plan to major in other subjects. Graduate Record Examination (GRE) scores of prospective teachers are lower than those of students majoring in other fields, and continue to drop.

We of all people understand that standardized–test scores present a picture of aptitude that is one–dimensional at best and deeply flawed at worst. But the Howley–Pendarvis book also looks at other indicators of teachers' academic interests and abilities. Again, the results are not encouraging. Prospective teachers took fewer liberal arts courses than did arts and sciences majors, and they took fewer higher–level courses in all subjects other than pedagogy. They quote from the authors of one study they review as follows:

> Teachers, as compared to arts and sciences graduates, take fewer hours in mathematics, English, physics, chemistry, economics, history, political sciences, sociology, other social sciences, foreign languages, philosophy, and other humanities.

Lastly, the Howleys and Pendarvis review studies that examine the reading habits of practicing teachers. While some show that teachers read about the same as most middle–class Americans (roughly eight books per year), others have found that teachers read considerably less than that, about three books per year. When teachers do read, the evidence shows, they are unlikely to be reading the kinds of journals that professionals typically follow to keep abreast of developments in their fields.

Blaming the Victim?

Having said all this, we do *not* believe that whatever is bad about our schools is the fault of lazy teachers. Rather, it's the inevitable outcome of the way that schools are structured and run that most of the best and the brightest will choose nearly any career path other than teaching.

This is borne out by the experience of programs like Teach for America and other alternative teacher recruitment pathways that seek to attract those who had trained for and embarked on other careers. The attrition rate of new teachers from these programs is very high, higher than that of conventional teacher training programs. Recruits from the "real world," no matter how well intentioned and strongly motivated, often find it impossible to accommodate themselves to the frustrating, trivialized nature of the piecework that constitutes much teaching today. It's not a question of money: New and prospective teachers are well aware of the poor pay they face, and choose to teach in spite of it. What drives the most competent and ambitious individuals from teaching is the lack of autonomy, the stultifying bureaucratic environment, and the limited career options that mark a life in public school teaching. A recent survey by the Department of Education of teachers who left the profession demonstrates this clearly. Among former public school teachers who cited "dissatisfaction with teaching as a career" as one of their main reasons for leaving the profession, only 0.7 percent cited "poor salary" as their main area of dissatisfaction, while almost 25 percent cited "inadequate support from the administration.[3] Another recent study found that private-school teachers were 50 percent more likely to be satisfied with their salaries than their public school counterparts, despite earning 30 percent less.

Over the past 150 years, one of the most popular responses to complaints about schools has been the tightening of teacher certification standards. During the nineteenth century, there were few if any teacher training programs, and states seldom required any specific preparation or qualifications of prospective teachers. Fortunately for students, teaching was one of the few career paths open to bright young women, and their presence, if generally unacknowledged in their own time, did much to boost the quality of teaching. In the early twentieth century, reformers like John Dewey and others began to press for a longer, more specific course of teacher preparation, and teacher's colleges proliferated. During the 1940s and '50s, states took over from local districts the right to set criteria for teacher certification, and began to require at least a bachelor's degree for teaching high school.

There are several reasons for the popularity of certification standards with state legislatures: They cost nothing; they implicitly place the onus for bad schools on teachers rather than on the system, and they bring more power to schools of education, which in turn rally support for the legislatures. Teachers themselves support tighter standards because they limit the number of people who can teach at any given moment. In fact, teacher's unions have historically been in the forefront of movements to tighten certification requirements, believing that this would raise teacher salaries and prestige. Of course, they want to be the ones controlling the certification process, and they are adamant that tighter standards should apply primarily to new teachers, not those already in the system. In 1989, Arthur E. Wise, President of the National Council for the Accreditation of Teacher Education, made a presentation to the National Education Association, the country's largest teacher's union, in which he outlined the organization's strategy concerning teacher certification and accreditation:

> You need to create coalitions...[many business] groups are concerned about the quality of American education; you have a partial answer to their concerns and that is how you need to present this issue....When you create coalitions, you need not always or should not always try to take credit for the accomplishments of those coalitions. Your motives are suspect....Let them take the credit....

> ...Standards and compensation are inextricably related. If there are standards for becoming a teacher, there is control over who is entitled to be a teacher. Supply and demand determines price. So it has always been, and so it will always be.

True Professionalization

The word professional is formally defined as someone involved in an occupation requiring advanced academic training, so when we look for professional teachers, we automatically think of entrance requirements. But we're probably looking in the wrong place. What really distinguishes professionals in our society is the autonomy they are granted. People don't tell lawyers or plumbers how to do their jobs; it's assumed they *know* how. If customers lose confidence in their plumber's or lawyer's abilities, they find a new plumber or a new lawyer. People don't tell their carpenters what to wear, or their accountants what hours they should work. We judge professionals by their ability to get the job done, by the outcome of their work. Since education is all about outcomes, we ought to want good teachers who will help us create good students, not simply those who have passed certain tests or taken certain courses.

Teacher support for certification has had little to do with improving the quality of teaching. At the same time as they have been pushing for greater control over an ever–stricter certification process, teachers have adamantly refused to have those same standards applied to the hundreds of thousands of teachers who are currently in classrooms. The combination of self–exemption, higher rather than lower hurdles for those who want to enter teaching, and the avoidance of performance standards serves to strengthen the status quo, not change it. The problem is not that it is too easy to become a teacher, or that the system fails to attract idealists. The problem is that conditions are such that, after a few years, too few people with opportunities to do anything else choose to remain in the field.

The Multiple National Curricula plan does not address teacher certification directly, but it would provide the numbers to judge where and when certification makes sense. For example, it's possible that biology teachers who have been to schools of education outperform those who haven't, but that history teachers perform about the same whether or not they're specially trained. It's possible that National Teaching Exam scores correlate with the ultimate performance of each teachers' students, but it's likely they won't (we'd bet our life savings on it).

We hope that decisions on such issues as certification, like all changes that would be considered under our plan, would be made through controlled experimentation. Should we open up our schools to more teachers like those recruited by Teach for America? Well, let's try a few and see how their students perform.

The Multiple National Curricula plan can spur a true professionalization of teaching, whereby increased responsibility is linked to increased reward, and where measurement and assessment are not shunned but embraced by teachers, administrators, and curriculum developers alike. In return for sharing their experiences, the plan will back participants up with the most comprehensive and meaningful data that education has ever yielded.

Local Control

In any decision–making process, the involvement of more people—each with a different but complementary set of interests—leads to more robust outcomes. In contrast to current systems where decisions about curricula, testing, and instructional materials are made at a relatively high level and include the participation of very few groups, our plan supports (but does not presuppose) a framework in which each school makes consequential decisions as to which curricula and texts it would use.

Again, the Multiple National Curricula model does not directly address who would pick curricula for a school. As we've said, different states would handle it differently. We strongly suspect that, over time, the accountability built into such a system would allow states to cede control over these issues to school districts (or for that matter, to department heads in schools) while monitoring their results carefully.

Most teachers, however, don't currently have the skills to analyze the data that would be generated under this proposal. Teachers are trained to teach what is set in front of them, not to evaluate it. They are trained to observe the behavior and responsiveness of their students, but not their own or that of their peers. They are taught to grade tests, but not how to create them. This is all part of a long historical process of "de–skilling" teachers, of making them into assembly–line workers whose job is to follow the directions of others rather than shape the conditions under which they work. The domination of classrooms by textbooks has been an integral part of this deprofessionalization, so much so that most teachers have come to depend on textbooks and would have difficulty teaching a class without them.

Evaluating Curricula

It's important that teachers receive training in the design and evaluation of instructional materials. Currently, this falls under the heading of "curriculum and instruction" in most schools of education, but ironically—or perhaps predictably—it is not taught to prospective teachers in any depth. Rather, it's the domain of a special class of mostly non–teaching school personnel who sit in central offices or publishing companies and develop or review materials that others will use. Yet it's hard to imagine too many skills that are more important to a truly professional teacher than the ability to assess and, if necessary, transform his or her own practice. Under the Multiple National Curriculum plan, schools of education are not the only places where this could be learned. States, districts, teachers' organizations, and curriculum developers could all fill this gap, training teachers from all over the country in the curricula they've developed and sponsored. Ultimately, the fees for such training could constitute a significant source of revenue for any of these groups.

As teachers gained expertise in curriculum design and evaluation they would broaden and deepen their skill base and become not only better instructors but more valuable employees. The expansion of the instructional materials market brought on by Multiple National Curricula would offer good teachers a parallel career path, much as university professors have been able to move back and forth between academia and industry. The accompanying increase in income, status, and autonomy would make teaching more attractive as a profession.

Of course, teachers would have a lot of help from the commercial world. As we've discussed, an industry would spring up around the numbers, much as one has grown up around the financial world. As the statistics start becoming available (for example, for a given demographic, which curricula correlate best with low drop–out rates or high performance in college, and which texts and supplemental materials work best with those curricula), they'll have better data to work with than any state or district education office has now.

Coalitions

The decentralized production of instructional materials under the Multiple National Curricula plan encourages the formation of many small entrepreneurial units composed of parents, teachers, administrators, curriculum specialists, testing companies and publishing/multimedia companies. These teams would create new tests and curricula, and refine old ones in response to classroom experience and competition, and produce the best materials to teach the curricula they create or adopt.

We expect a process analogous to what happened in the U.S. auto industry when the Japanese companies came into the market. Not only did the elimination of manufacturing defects become a priority, but the new car cycle was shortened dramatically. Less dramatically, Snapple's success quickly brought us Fruitopia from Coca Cola.

Unlike the current system, under which one or two companies win big by persuading a few people on a board in Texas or California, the proponents of curricula or materials under our system have to go out and persuade many people—teachers, administrators, parents—in many different places that their course of study or their set of materials really is the best. Since the decisions are being made all the time by various groups, new editions would appear more often, as opposed to the current five- to seven-year edit cycle, which mirrors the adoption cycle of many states.

This does not mean that state or district education offices would become irrelevant. The experience they're acquired over the years in making decisions about curricula will enable them to play an important educative and consultative role as we make the transition from centralized to decentralized control. When that transformation is complete, those agencies will have become resources, pools of expertise on which schools and others who want to develop curricula and materials can draw for guidance and support. Thus the state retains an important role, but rather than issue edicts it serves to support decision-making by others.

Schools of education would undergo a similar conversion. As high schools themselves become the driving force behind experimentation and innovation, the present-day schools of education would find a different niche. They will become involved in more and more partnerships with businesses, PTAs, school districts, and teachers associations seeking to improve materials or to develop new ones. As a new sense of distributed expertise spreads and becomes accepted (and this may take some time, since universities are among the most conservative of all educational institutions), we expect to see an increase in collaboration across disciplinary boundaries. A nascent field of information design, drawing on the skills of graphic artists, psychologists, computer scientists, semioticians, and sociologists, has much to offer departments of curriculum and instruction as they carve out distinctive and productive functions for themselves in the evolving institution of formal education.

As for teacher preparation, there is little reason why most of it can't be distributed among other university departments like psychology, sociology, statistics, and the like, assuming it needs to take place in universities at all.

Ongoing Research

When educational research is conducted today, it is almost always on a small scale. It is seldom experimental in design because schools are not about to let researchers turn their classrooms upside down "just to see how this turns out." At the same time, it's very difficult to do a widely accepted retrospective study of something as complex as schooling because of the difficulty in correcting for (or even identifying) all the variables that might account for a given outcome. Academic studies of education bear an additional burden in that, although their intention is generally descriptive, they are often recruited in a political effort to prescribe, to persuade, to suggest how things ought to be done. Since any change in education policy involves a change in the way money is spent and the kinds of goals and values that are articulated, there will always be opponents ready to criticize the premises, the methods, or the conclusions of any study, no matter how well constructed. The result is that very little is ever widely agreed upon.

The evaluation of teaching and curriculum should not be an isolated academic exercise but rather a commonplace practice of educators working in partnership with one another, with curriculum designers, with researchers. Teaching and learning are complex, messy social processes that cannot be abstracted, distilled, or isolated from the environment in which they are practiced. You cannot learn about the classroom outside of the classroom.

The Multiple National Curricula model would introduce and support this sort of research in schools. Once schools are assessed on the basis of the academic value that they add, they would begin to test different tools and techniques in the hope of improving those outcomes. More importantly, they would pay closer attention to research going on in other schools, so as to build on others' successes. If a department is weak, a school would find itself on the defensive: "Why aren't you changing things? Why aren't you using the methods that XYZ school is using with such great results?" In such an environment, it's much easier to experiment—even if you sometimes fail—than to defend something that isn't working.

Distributed Research

The combination of the school prospectus with Multiple National Curricula would give teachers and administrators the tools they need to conduct meaningful research, both formal and informal. Such research, emerging from schools and classrooms, would have greater credibility than what currently comes out of universities. And it would be done simultaneously by many people with diverse institutional interests and perspectives that would tend to balance out one another's parochial interests.

If university or agency–based research is like a centrally planned economy, then collaborative, distributed, school–based investigation is like the market. When information is broadly accessible and the decision–making process is chaotic, uncoordinated, and widely dispersed, the final product is likely to be more useful, more flexible, and more durable. Of course, this principle—which lies at the heart of both democracy and market economies—is as antithetical to bureaucracy as it can be.

This is not to say that there is no place for the contributions that a university can make to schools. Advances in information design and management, developmental psychology, interactive technologies, and organizational theory often originate there, although generally not within schools of education. The university provides an environment in which policy can be formulated and basic research carried out, and it has the administrative resources to coordinate large projects. But given its notorious indifference to quality of instruction, its self–sufficient insularity, and the fact that it never deals with kids, it is perhaps the worst place to train aspiring teachers.

The return of research to the classroom would end a vicious degenerative cycle in which teachers are not trained to evaluate new developments or current practice because they have little chance of being able to initiate change, and where they face little likelihood of being given that kind of authority because they are not trained or equipped for it. Here is a chance for a new positive cycle to replace the old. Teachers and administrators, responding to parental initiatives as well as their own, would begin to carry out their own studies in collaboration with other schools. The ability to think critically, to innovate, and to evaluate would become increasingly central to a reinvigorated craft of teaching. The acquisition and refinement of these skills would become the main substance of teacher preparation, whether conducted in schools of education or elsewhere. Certification requirements, if they still existed, would be restructured to reflect the importance of these new skills, and the thousands of bright, dedicated people who have historically been reluctant to enter teaching because of its stultifying insistence on convention and rule–following would be attracted by its increasing professionalization.

The Freedom to Be Different

After a short time under our plan teachers, schools, and curricula would begin to differentiate themselves from one another. Some would clearly be more suited to certain situations than others. Others would be all–around performers. Some wouldn't work very well at all. The data on curriculum outcomes would be detailed enough to guide the improvement of those that seem worth saving. Since curricula would be standardized and distributed across many schools and geographic regions, support networks would form among users to foster improvements. These networks would be supported by curriculum sponsors, testing companies, and instructional materials publishers, all of whom would have a vested interest in student success at the classroom level. There would likely be workshops sponsored by developers and taught by the star teachers of each program, who would be well paid for their contributions. The modest cost of attending these workshops might be borne by individual teachers or by their institutions, just as professional development is handled in other fields.

In such an environment, teachers would be seen less and less as baby–sitting textbook readers and more and more like frontline managers of curricular innovation, while principals would gain recognition for developing innovative programs of support that foster excellence among their staff.

We Are All the Same

In order for this to happen, states and school boards must loosen their grip on schools' throats, and start treating professional educators as such. Since the turn of the century, all levels of the education establishment from state school officers to local boards to teachers' unions have chosen to champion uniformity, predictability, and reproducibility over inspiration, excellence, and innovation.

The obsession with uniformity manifests itself in a whole array of practices that are plainly irrational if the goal is to support educational excellence for as many students as possible. It's what gives us the notion that history classes, for example, must be as long as English classes; that each subject must occupy no more and no less than one school–year; that teachers and principals must be paid the same regardless of their contribution to student learning; and that schools in poor areas with no tax base must be financed through the same mechanism as schools in rich areas. None of these deeply ingrained practices has anything whatever to do with learning or even, at bottom, with functional equivalence. There is no equivalence (let alone, sense) in treating widely varying situations as if they were identical, or in attempting to make them so.

What About the Unions?

As practitioners of an underpaid and undervalued trade, teachers have historically depended on collective bargaining to secure fair treatment. In a system that was consciously modeled on the factory, with teachers as the production–line workers carrying out the orders of higher–ups, collective bargaining made sense. Since it was inconceivable that teachers would have any meaningful control over what they did or how they did it, unions could at least enforce some minimum standards for working conditions and salary against a management that simply looked to work teachers as hard as possible while paying them as little as they could.

Unions were formed to support the "professionalization" of teaching (the NEA was formed in 1857), yet the result has been to promote its opposite. While teachers' unions hold in common with professional associations the desire to promote the well–being of their members, the differences in their approach and assumptions say a great deal about the pervasive lack of true professionalism that characterizes teaching today. Professionals—as we commonly use the term (lawyers, doctors, accountants, scientists, and the like)—don't typically embrace collective bargaining or rigid work rules. They do not seek to avoid performance–based judgments of their members. They expect that with their mastery of a specialized body of knowledge and practice comes the discretion to set the terms of their employment. Professionals are not wage laborers: They do not sell themselves but rather a product or outcome for which they are personally responsible.

Teachers' unions have strenuously resisted this kind of accountability. That's understandable. Given that teachers are rarely given the discretion to practice according to their best understanding and experience of how children learn, it would be unfair to hold them accountable for the outcome.

As parents and administrators become more comfortable with quantifiable results, there will be increasing pressure to tie compensation and autonomy to performance. Pressure will also come from top-performing teachers, who will resent having their salaries tied to the average. The movement toward merit pay is not inconsistent with unions; professional athletes have unions and yet still receive widely disparate salaries.

Accept-No-Substitute Teachers

However the pay scales are determined, the pressure to improve poorly performing departments would become overwhelming. The unions' response to that pressure will be critical in determining their future.

A teacher might be getting terrible results for many reasons. He could have untrainable students (try *that* out on parents), the class might be too large, the curriculum chosen might be a poor match with the students or teacher, the textbook might be terrible, the teacher might have been inadequately trained, or he *might* be a terrible teacher.

A smart principal would examine the evidence. How do these students do in other classes? What do they think of the teacher? (Ask the kids? Sure. The Princeton Review does it at the end of each course, and we get great information about our staff.) What is the class size? Do other teachers at the school have better results with the same curricula? What other curricula might be a better fit for students like this? Is the teacher willing to retrain?

If the union helps speed this sort of analysis by training its members, it would be an important ally of the school and parents. If not, it will be seen by parents as a major force working against the education of their kids—not an enviable position.

Rather than being seen as protectors of mediocrity, teachers' unions will have the opportunity to position themselves in the forefront of educational reform by supporting the professionalization of their members. This could take several forms: Ongoing workshops to develop the critical evaluative skills teachers would need to become full curricular partners; the sponsorship of innovative classroom programs developed by teachers themselves; or the development of working relationships with colleges, textbook producers, and testing companies that give teachers a strong voice in the continual evolution of teaching and learning.

Ideally, unions would evolve into guilds, associations that protect their members' interests while certifying that every member is capable of practicing his or her trade to a demonstrable standard of quality. Teachers who were unable to do so would be offered further training or risk losing their union sponsorship and the prestige that would accompany it. This kind of certification by ability has nothing to do with where or even whether someone graduated from a school of education. Such an approach would be better for teachers, better for students, and better for schools.

CHAPTER 10

School Choice

What a Market Needs

Of the many reform proposals floated over the past decade, the ones that have most captured the public imagination involve some form of what has come to be known, somewhat misleadingly, as "school choice." There are many variations on the theme—from choosing only among public schools to using state–financed vouchers to pay tuition at private schools—with a range of gradations in between. Still, the basic premise is the same: If public school students are free to attend any one of a number of schools, and consequently no school had a captive base of students, then market pressures will force schools to work harder to retain clients. Those that failed to make themselves attractive to students and parents would be forced to close.

It is easy to see why this idea has become so popular. It is conceptually straightforward. It doesn't require much, if any, increased expenditure on schools. It places education within the same market framework as most other aspects of American life. Finally, it places the burden of school improvement on the schools themselves, implicitly absolving parents and legislatures of responsibility for the condition of their schools.

Supply-Side Schools

School choice was first proposed by the economist Milton Friedman in 1962.[1] He envisioned a system of government-financed vouchers that parents could redeem at the school of their choice. The underlying motive was to break what he regarded as a state monopoly on the education of children.

Friedman did not think of choice as a tool for improving schools (at the time, schools were not widely seen as needing systemic improvement). His main concern was ideological. He considered the idea of government–sponsored public schooling to be deeply out of sync with the marketplace values and mechanisms on which the country was founded. Further, Friedman made the compelling argument that a system without choice allows wealthier people to send their kids to private school while forcing the poor to remain within a system that may not serve them well.

The idea was not very popular in its own time or during the twenty years that followed. Friedman's proposal went directly against the grain of a three-hundred-year-old tradition of common schooling, and a one-hundred-year tradition of financing those schools from public taxes. At a time when the country was actively and painfully struggling to replace a segregated and unequal system of schooling for rich and poor and black and white, the idea of removing the state entirely from the picture seemed irresponsible to most people.

At bottom, though, retooling the very bases of public education looked like a solution in search of a problem, a fix for something that wasn't broken. For the next two decades, the societal consensus was in fact the opposite of what Friedman thought, that the state ought to play a greater, not lesser, role in both funding and control of public education.

Gathering Steam

This consensus disintegrated during the early 1980s. The Reagan administration tied together the growing dissatisfaction with both public schools and large government, and pushed for the distribution of publicly funded vouchers that parents could use to pay for private or parochial schools. At the same time, some education policy analysts were beginning to wonder whether many of the problems with the public schools didn't stem from the fact that they were monopolies, essentially assured of their existence regardless of how poorly they served their clientele. School choice seemed like one possible solution.

Since then, school choice has brought together some interesting bed-fellows, both in support and opposition. Some proponents see choice as the last hope for revitalizing public education, while others see it as an opportunity to dismantle public schools entirely. Among opponents are those who feel that marketplace mechanisms are anathema to the egalitarian values embodied in common schools, those who think it is a simplistic panacea, and those with a vested interest in the present system of unaccountability. Like the question of school integration a generation ago, school choice has become a sort of crime boss of education policy, a figure that all reform proposals must acknowledge and treat with respect, whatever stance they take.

It's easy to talk about markets if you were sent to a good school and attended a fine college. To some opponents of school choice, it seems painfully clear that the function of all markets—whether of soap, cars, or schooling—is to distribute the best products to those who can afford to pay the most for them. They feel that it is a central obligation of a democracy to prevent markets from forming in something that is the basis of success in our society.

Reasonable people disagree about nearly everything concerning schools, especially the values they should embody. Rather than taking a stand on the moral or practical value of school choice, therefore, we confine ourselves to an examination of the actual mechanisms of making choices about schools and of the consequences when such choices are made. The Multiple National Curricula plan neither requires nor rejects school choice. In fact, it can be used to bolster either position. In this respect, the plan is once again a neutral tool.

Whose Choice?

There are several questions confronting anyone looking at school reform proposals that employ choice: On what basis will choices be made? Who chooses whom? From what may one choose? What is the consequence of choice for good schools? For bad schools? For rich schools? For poor schools?

As some proponents of choice will tell you (Friedman among them), a system of school choice already exists in this country. Rich people can choose to send their kids to any number of private schools, or to move to the district with the public schools of their choosing. Private schools and wealthy school districts each have carefully cultivated reputations, spread by word of mouth among real-estate agents, parents of graduates, and the press (and by myth and legend). One of the most widely relied-upon indices of quality is also one of the simplest: expense. It is nearly axiomatic

In an efficient market in which each action taken by participants reflects the sum of all that is known at the time, each decision adds new information. In an inefficient market, of which education is a paragon, choices may just as easily represent misinformation, whim, and wishful thinking.

that schools and districts with the best reputations are also the most expensive or have the highest property taxes.

If school choice were instituted today (and let's assume for a moment that it is a limited form of public school choice that doesn't involve tuition vouchers for private schools), students would migrate to nearby schools based in large part on such things as the standings of sports teams, the extravagance of senior class trips, or the physical plant.

Choice Is Not Prime

Ideally, a well-made choice would achieve an appropriate match between student and school and so benefit both. But even when operating under ideal conditions, there are real limits to these benefits, both for those directly involved and for the educational system generally. First, such a process would simply anoint those schools that are already commonly thought to be doing well. If it is possible to predict in advance which schools will be chosen, then the process adds no new information.

Second, choice does nothing to help schools that are not already considered good get better. All that a crowded, dangerous inner–city school can see about Andover or Scarsdale High School is their well-kept buildings and small class sizes. It has no access to what, if anything, is going on in those well–appointed classrooms that helps kids learn, and the nature of the do–or–die competition fostered by choice gives schools no incentive whatsoever to share their secrets with one another.

Finally, public schools as we know them have very little leeway to be different from one another, making "choice" by and large symbolic. Thus, when school choice has been tried in places like Minnesota, parents have tended to choose schools based more on proximity than on any other factor. While some regard this as evidence that parents are incapable of making rational decisions about what is best for their kids, it can also be seen as a sensible response to alternatives that present no real choice at all, and no intelligent criteria by which to choose.

As an abstraction, school choice has strengths and weaknesses. Under our present system, however, with its enforced uniformity (other than in funding) and lack of meaningful data about school outcomes with which to inform the selection process, it is largely irrelevant. While establishing a regime of choice would soothe the nerves of those like Friedman who believe that choice is *a priori* desirable, it is difficult to see how, given the overarching organizational structure within which schools operate, it would lead to much systemic improvement.

Sink or Swim

School choice is presented as a two–pronged instrument by its advocates: It provides more options to parents, and it provides an extremely persuasive incentive for schools to please their clientele. If a school is unchosen by large numbers of kids for any significant period of time, it shuts down.

Those who see choice as a means to foster school improvement maintain that this sink–or–swim market pressure will force bad schools to become good schools. It should, as Samuel Johnson said about imminent death by hanging, concentrate the mind wonderfully. Unless you provide a mechanism for bad schools to improve, however, school choice is merely an executioner, and a cowardly one at that. We could identify and close bad schools today if we wanted to, without engaging in a masquerade of change.

This is the aspect of choice that is generally glossed over by its supporters. In order for bad schools to turn into good schools a great many things need to occur. All of these things require time, and many require money—commodities conspicuous in their absence from most choice plans. Good, responsive teachers and administrators need to be attracted and retained. Central authorities need to stand aside long enough for schools to try new ideas and find those that work. Buildings may need to be renovated to be fit for human occupancy. Support structures for ongoing training and mentoring must be in place to foster teacher development. If all those things were available so that bad schools had the chance to become good schools, then choice would make sense. But if all those things were available to bad schools, then choice would be unnecessary. While you may or may not support school choice as an abstract ideal, in the real world it seems clear that school choice would be a more powerful tool if schools were allowed to differentiate themselves, and if weak schools were provided the resources with which to improve. The Multiple National Curricula plan provides for just that.

I'll Vouch for You If You'll Vouch for Me

The most radical implementations of school choice would have the state provide students with vouchers that fund attendance at any school of a student's choosing, public or private. Some plans provide for vouchers that pay only a portion of most private school tuition (parents would pay the rest out–of–pocket) and allow schools to charge whatever tuition they like. Under other plans, schools could only participate by accepting the state voucher as payment of full tuition. California, birthplace of the tax revolt movements that led to drastic cutbacks in local school funding in the 1980s, is now experimenting with a plan that grants tuition vouchers worth $3400 to parents who enroll their children in private schools, as well as a plan for choice within the public schools. Not surprisingly, local television stations there have been flooded with commercials for schools seeking to attract or retain students.

The explicit purpose of voucher programs is to make it easier for students to attend private schools. While some people favor this because they are overtly hostile to the idea of state–run schools, most of its advocates feel that private schools will be able to respond more innovatively to educational problems, and that this innovation will then diffuse into the public schools. Since such proposals necessarily involve basic questions of school financing, we consider them to be mostly outside the scope of this book. Nevertheless we can touch on a few points of consideration.

First, any such proposal self–evidently takes money out of the public school system as those dollars follow students who are most desirable to private schools. Private school "choice" programs are somewhat misnamed, since they offer students the option not of attending any school they like, but of *applying* to it. Schools retain the right to select the students they will admit, which means the first few years of any such program will witness a massive sorting of public school students into two groups: those who are relatively easy and inexpensive to educate, who will leave the public system, and those who are more difficult and more expensive to educate, who will remain. In a very short time, the public schools will become concentrated with the most troubled and troubling students, the rest having been cherry–picked by private schools.

Expensive students include anyone with learning or behavior problems, those whose first language is not English, those who are chronically ill, and those who take subjects like science that require smaller classes and more equipment than, say, math.

Second, plans like this amount to a subsidy for private schools. As in other industries, this will drive prices up. Let's say you run a private school charging $9,000 right now. If the government agrees to pay $4,000, your first thought might be to lower your tuition to $5,000 leaving parents with a $1,000 balance to pay. But there is no reason to do that. Anyone who currently goes to your school can afford the full $9,000, and even if you only lower the price to $7,000, you will still attract new students. Most likely, you will lower your tuition a bit, and spend the rest in higher salaries, new computers, and higher overhead.

Plans like California's, where schools can charge what they like and families make up the difference between tuition and the amount of the voucher, also ensure that your school won't be besieged by poor kids who might frighten your regular clientele, since most poor families will not be able to raise the necessary $5,000 every year. In one stroke you make more money, your families pay less, and "undesirables" are excluded, all with the blessing of the state.

Ruining Private Schools

Plans that require schools to accept the voucher as full payment are somewhat better. However, anyone who has taken Economics 101 knows that a price ceiling would encourage private schools to cut corners, or charge extra for such things as extracurricular sports or chemistry lab materials (or anything else not required of them by the state).

In either case, the state would be required to heavily regulate the private school market to discourage fraud and corner–cutting. It would have to guarantee that private schools were subject to the same constraints as the public schools in terms of curricular offerings, length of school day, assessment procedures, nutritional value of lunches, teacher hiring standards, and everything else that makes a school a school. Not only would this oversight be cumbersome, expensive, and prone to corruption, it would eliminate the capacity for difference and innovation that is alleged to be the main virtue of voucher plans. The inescapable need for direct oversight would make private schools more like public schools, not vice versa, as supporters assert.

Choice plans, then, run into many of the same walls that schools face now. Since weak schools would not be given the tools to rehabilitate themselves, they would die rather than improve. Since schools would be forced to be similar to one another, and since no real data would exist about their educational quality, parents would end up making the choice to keep their kids in the closest school. Finally, plans that effectively require families to supplement the state voucher would very likely cripple what remains of the public school system, further diminishing what educational opportunity remains for disadvantaged students who cannot afford the difference between the state voucher and tuition at a decent school.

Other Than That, Mrs. Lincoln, How Was the Play?

We are not against the *concept* of choice. All else being equal, having a choice is better for an individual than not having one. In terms of its ability to improve everyone's public education, however, choice is only meaningful if good information exists to support the process of choosing and if competitors have the ability to change themselves in response to a changing environment.

In giving parents real information about the education that each available school is offering, through the school's prospectus and through the industry we see growing up around the data, the Multiple National Curricula plan provides the basis for a reasonable marketplace. Parents could pick schools on more than a hunch. In giving teachers and administrators feedback on their classroom and school–level performance, the plan makes it much more likely that weak schools will have the chance to repair themselves before being abandoned. Finally, if our plan is successful in restoring individual schools' ability to determine their own curricular goals and how to pursue them, it will allow them to differentiate themselves, making choice that much more meaningful to parents and students, and ultimately to colleges and employers.

If you already like the concept of school choice, the Multiple National Curricula plan provides the tools to implement it in the most effective manner possible. If you are opposed to school choice, you can use these same tools to improve the public schools to which students are assigned. Regardless of your views (or ours) on the subject of school choice, schools and students are better off with the Multiple National Curricula plan than they are without it.

Could This Actually Happen?

The Immovable Object

This is a chapter you won't find in most books on education reform. As good as many of the ideas floating around the education world are, they will be implemented only if the head of American education enacts them. For better or for worse, there is no head of American education.

The long history of school organization in America does not incline people towards optimism. As we discussed in chapter two, despite a tremendous quantity of rhetoric, public schools were not designed to be places of learning first and foremost. Excellence was never the primary goal. Teachers and administrators have never been trained as professionals or permitted to work as such. Complex cultural traits like anti–intellectualism, a broad streak of indifference to the needs of children, and (in this century) a rejection of civic communalism have all contributed to the present condition of our public schools. It is foolish and self–serving to imagine that any plan for school reform can by itself transform these aspects of our society, which are themselves major contributors to the problems schools face.

Nor is the marketplace alone the answer to our problems. To the extent that market mechanisms have been permitted to operate in schooling they have worked as markets will tend to, allocating the best products and services to those with the most money to spend while leaving the rest of us with a few alternatives whose quality ranges from mediocre to awful. The scarce commodities—good teachers and wealthy students—tend to migrate to that subset of schools (small and growing smaller) that can treat them well and provide tolerable working conditions like toilets that flush, reasonable class sizes, protection from violence, and at least a modicum of respect for the complex social processes of teaching and learning.

This book has purposely avoided discussing questions of school finance and equity because we believe they are insufficient to explain why schools don't work as well as they might. Multiple National Curricula can play a big part in solving several problems with American education, regardless of how it is financed. It resolves much of the tension between local, state, and national control over curriculum, and properly integrates assessment and instruction. Such a program, as we've explained, can introduce accountability and responsiveness to our schools, while giving teachers and principals the tools and the freedom to choose their own goals and work as professionals.

Originally, we believed such a system could be set up by a national committee. Such an organization (which could be government-funded, an independent foundation, or the College Board itself) would grant a new curriculum its seal of approval. Parents, we reasoned, would force their high schools to choose from among approved curricula.

But who would establish such a committee? And who are these people who would decide what our students would be taught? By what means would they approve curricula? What leverage would they possess to encourage schools to sign on? Most importantly, how would we know whether these curricula were any good, or if teachers and students were actually teaching and learning them? Would there be pointless multiple-choice tests attached (like the National Assessment of Educational Progress) that wasted class time and asked kids to try their hardest, while knowing that they would never even *see* their scores, much less be judged by them?

We need to create a system of national curricula without a self–serving bureaucracy that surfaces from its torpor every few years to complain about the sorry state of our kids. We need to develop a framework of accountability that would keep everyone's feet to the fire for all four years of high school without making kids, teachers, or administrators into harried drones.

The Customer

A few insights helped us find our solution. The first is that most schools do not perceive their clients to be students and parents, and in fact spend a great deal of energy insulating themselves from parents. Rather, they see themselves as serving the businesses that hire their graduates, the colleges that accept them, and the legislative–bureaucratic regime that foots the bill.   At some point in the future, particularly if Multiple National Curricula are adopted, parents might have more meaningful impact than they do now, and that would be good. But that's not how things stand, and so pressure to change will have to come more from the businesses and colleges than from kids and parents.

The second insight was that assessment must be tied closely to curriculum. That is, teaching, learning, and testing have to be related to one another in some meaningfully organic fashion as reciprocal instruments of curricular goals. "Minimum competency" tests promote minimum learning; tests should set goals to strive for. Rather than be limited to laundry lists of multiple–choice "cultural literacy" factoids, the system should accommodate essay, portfolio, oral, computer–adaptive, or any other kind of tests that could measure deeper understanding. Finally, for tests to be worthwhile, they should be administered in a predictable, replicable manner, and the consequences of their scores should be important enough to get students' attention.

The Speech

The first hurdle is to get a few top colleges to change their admissions criteria. We have used the President of Harvard as a straw man to make the point that our proposal does not assume a mass uprising or federal intervention. It needs only a handful of people to push with moderate force on a long lever. They don't need to make a burdensome investment of time or money, and may act as much from self–interest as from altruism. If it isn't the Ivies, it could be NACAC (the National Association of College Admissions Counselors), the NCAA (National Collegiate Athletics Association), a large group of small colleges, or a small group of state-college systems.

> History has demonstrated that a group of colleges working together can essentially set the agenda for public education. As we have described, the NEA Committee of Ten, which gave us the Carnegie unit 100 years ago, was headed by then-Harvard President Charles Elliot. The recommendations of that committee fundamentally defined the character of schooling right up until today.

The second hurdle is to get the other colleges to follow suit. If these new curriculum–bound assessments are accepted by only one or two well–known colleges, they will quickly disappear. But we believe that other colleges will join the movement out of enlightened self–interest. Admissions officers are currently being pressured to admit students according to superficial, formulaic procedures that are just as well handled by computer (in fact, large colleges increasingly are cutting out the middleman and just letting computers make the decision). The Multiple National Curricula plan is an opportunity for admissions officers to regain control of the admissions process by working with their institutions to select acceptable curricula and acceptable scores on those assessments.

The testing and textbook companies are not obstacles, as they stand to gain the most financially from this proposal. Both groups will experience fiercer competition, but the expansion of the market and the increased capital that will flow into education should make these companies strong allies in bringing Multiple National Curricula to life. The Educational Testing Service (ETS), however much we mock them, is well situated to be the testing company of choice under our system. They already give their tests nationally, they have credibility—perhaps too much—with colleges, businesses, politicians, and schools, and they have the capital to spend on this new generation of tests (1993 revenues were $349 million).

We have no doubt that many existing testing and textbook companies would compete aggressively, and that new players would enter the market in droves, especially in the areas of instructional materials and curriculum design. Since the administration of the tests will be handled by the schools (as is now generally the case for tests like the SAT, APs, and ACT), and since many niche markets will flourish, it will not require a tremendous amount of capital to administer national tests or market instructional materials. This is an aspect of education where choice and competition have virtually no downside, and the benefits of that competition accrue to governments, schools, teachers, and parents alike. We will very quickly see a much greater variety of materials available from diverse suppliers, all competing to meet the schools' present needs while creating innovative products for the future.

Finally, since all national curricula would be linked to and accompanied by tests, and vice versa, assessment and curricula expertise would cross–pollinate one another, advancing the state of both arts exponentially. The unproductive cycle of blame—in which testing companies, textbook companies, and curriculum–and–instruction people endlessly point fingers at one another—would end.

A Million Flowers

How many distinct curricula should there be? Ideally, enough in each subject to ensure real competition among them and real choices for teachers and students. It is desirable for schools to be able to make fairly fine–grained choices based on content, goals, method of assessment, and so on. This would not be possible with just a few curricula to choose from, and innovation would quickly wither. On the other hand, it would be counterproductive to have so many curricula that colleges would have no clue what test scores from each signified. That would prevent a valid basis for comparison, refinement, and improvement.

Fortunately, the Multiple National Curricula model will tend toward a kind of self–managing diversity. Colleges choosing the tests they will accept, and states, districts, and schools deciding what to offer their students, will dampen any wild profusion of curricula, while increased autonomy for teachers and principals combined with market incentives for curriculum developers will tend to encourage it. If enough teachers or parents feel there is no curriculum available that addresses their needs, there will be plenty of developers willing to create one for them. Similarly, a teacher or other independent developer with a really worthwhile idea for teaching art history or solid geometry should be able to find enough supporters among university faculty, high-school teachers, parents, or independent curriculum evaluators that a few schools and colleges can be persuaded to try it for a while. We believe colleges and schools that agree to offer or accept a given curriculum ought to make enough of an initial time commitment so bugs can be worked out and useful data gathered, perhaps three years or so. Ultimately, though, unpopular curricula used by only a few schools will probably be killed off by the burdens of administering and reporting national exams every year, or more importantly, by the inability to collate enough diverse student responses to determine whether the curricula were any good.

There are three million high-school students studying Algebra I this year; fifty curricula would allow comparisons among 60,000 of them, a lot more than enough for statistical validity.

The need to have a curriculum offered by a given number of institutions is more a technical than a policy limitation. If advances in administrative technology or statistical analysis permit sponsors to offer valid assessments on a very small scale, there is no reason why schools and colleges need shy away from curricula that are offered or accepted by just a few schools.

The Feds

The Department of Education, through the National Center for Education Statistics, should play a role in the education universe that is analogous to that of the Securities and Exchange Commission in the financial world, making sure that everyone has access to useful, reliable information with which to support their decisions. This is an appropriate role for government and is nonpartisan to the core.

If schools and colleges have signed on, the federal government will probably be pressured to assist in just this manner. The Multiple National Curricula proposal is consistent with the current mood of government: It creates free markets subject to intelligent regulation; it gives control to local communities; it makes good use of emerging information infrastructures; and it can readily exploit new technologies. Government oversight—but not policy making—will stimulate constructive spending on education and encourage the money to flow among a much greater number of parties, including new curriculum developers, teacher-consultants, new testing companies, new instructional designers, and materials developers. Ultimately, money will tend to flow most to those whose work leads to the best educational outcomes, rather than to those who are most firmly entrenched, as is the case now.

At the end of the day, however, it is not a real problem if the federal government initially does nothing, or only reacts. If the process evolves without oversight, flaws and abuses will develop and be exposed, giving the government ample opportunity to step in. Only if the government insists on specifying what constitutes a single national curricula (which we think highly unlikely for all of the reasons discussed earlier) would its involvement be detrimental.

The Kids

There is a legitimate concern that the kind of national assessments supported by our plan would create performance pressure on students even worse than that placed on kids in Japanese schools. Making schools accountable is fine—making them grim factories is not. We think we have struck a pretty good balance.

In terms of college admissions, for example, quantifiable academic performance now counts for about 60 percent toward a decision to admit or reject a student. Of that, the student's grades and test scores each count for about half. Assuming that recipe continues to apply after the adoption of Multiple National Curricula, a student who has taken fifteen high-school courses by the time a college reviews her application would know that each final test score will count only two percent toward that decision. The difference between an 85 and a 95 on any particular test would be 2 percent of the total decision—enough to notice but not enough to drive someone crazy. It would certainly constitute less—and less destructive—pressure than the SAT does now.

Let's also remember that not all assessment pressure is the same. Decontextualized tests like the SAT, which are intentionally unrelated in form and content to what students spend their time learning in school, are far more intimidating and disruptive than exams given in the normal course of learning. Tests that proceed organically from their curricula are less threatening and less alienating to most kids, especially when, as will be the case here, students know in advance how and on what they will be tested.

The High Schools

Will the education establishment—particularly the teachers and principals in individual schools—embrace or reject this plan? Their active support is not critical to the plan's success; most teachers today revile the SAT, but a million people take it every year anyway. While no one can mandate that teachers be enthusiastic participants in the re–design of education, things will work a lot better if those who must implement it also support it. Excited teachers and administrators can do amazing things even without active support from the bureaucracy above them.

Support from the private prep schools will not be a problem. As long as the colleges hold firm in their embrace of Multiple National Curricula, prep schools will actively participate. Parochial schools have similar incentives, and their financial backing and network of affiliation place them in an excellent position to create their own curricula. Schools operated as public/private hybrids—like those of Education Alternatives, Inc., a for–profit firm that operates public schools for local municipalities in several locations around the country—will be in a similar position.

As important as private and parochial schools are, the aim of our proposal is the invigoration and redefinition of public schooling. We must consider realistically whether public education—and by that we mean both the institution as a whole and the individuals who serve it in their various capacities as teachers, principals, administrators, policy makers, and legislators—has both the incentive and the capacity to transform itself radically.

In each public school system there will only need to be a few people who buy into the idea of teaching one of the available national curricula (or creating a new one) to get the ball rolling. They could be at the state, regional, or local level. They could be voters, legislators, educators, or parents. They might sign on because they want to make selective colleges available to their students, or they want to introduce more accountability into their schools, or they want their students to have access to the tools and textbooks springing up around the new national curricula. Once the alternative example is set, we believe others will follow.

We know that large, entrenched bureaucracies by their very nature resist change. We know that the first imperative of any organization (like any organism) is to perpetuate itself. And yet, all of our experience tells us that as the momentum builds, the high schools will join—especially if they consider the alternatives.

The Times, They Are a Changin'

This book was not written in a vacuum. Schools are under enormous, unprecedented pressure to submit to radical change. Some of this pressure takes reassuringly familiar (if ultimately wrongheaded) forms, like the calls from legislators or teachers' unions to tighten certification requirements, lengthen the school year, or introduce a national curriculum. Some of it is both radical and sensible, like Charter Schools experiments, Oregon's proposal to abolish the Carnegie unit, or Michigan's abandonment of property taxes as a means of paying for its schools.

These calls for change reflect the development of a remarkable transideological consensus among business leaders, political analysts, social scientists, parents, school experts, and economists regarding the need for fundamental change. Attention is being given to proposals that would have been unthinkable a generation ago. Vouchers, school choice, the abolition of school boards, allowing students to take college classes for high school credit, recruitment of teachers from outside schools of education, the use of private firms to run public schools, are all being tried throughout the country.

The public school establishment is coming to recognize that it must change, must experiment with alternatives to business–as–usual if it is to survive into the next century. This does not mean that school boards, unions, state agencies, and untouchable administrators will not fight like hell to maintain the status quo. They will, but they will lose. Just as our health-care and welfare systems will not live out the decade in their current form, neither will our school systems. We can't say for certain what form the change will take, but it will come.

The school establishment—both the system and the individual schools themselves—is approaching an imminent organizational crisis. This vulnerability makes the system particularly permeable to radical ideas. The danger, of course, is that in the rush to change but at the same time cling to what is familiar, harmful schemes like a single national curricula will find favor, just as the fall of state capitalism in Eastern Europe opened the door to rabid nationalism and rising fascism. What's needed to avoid grasping at the most attractive straw of the moment is some consensus on goals and the development of tools to meet them.

But, as we saw in the chapter on national curricula, it will probably be impossible in a society as diverse as ours to reach consensus on goals, if by "goals" we mean a uniform prescription for what and how every child must learn. Further, the tools needed to achieve such a goal—standardization at the lowest and highest levels, all–powerful central education committees, and the ultimate de–skilling of the art of teaching—would probably be unacceptable to most Americans.

The kinds of goals that are achievable, on the other hand, are those that themselves enable as many other goals as possible. Achieving the general goal of accountability, for example, would then make it possible for schools to attain more specific, local goals set down by parents, school boards, or state officials. This accountability in turn would make possible the still higher goal of *responsiveness*, in which schools are involved in an ongoing dialogue with those they serve, rather than simply being called to account every once in a while. Without accountability, however, other goals are not achievable.

New Tools

Goals and tools that are mutually supportive constitute an extremely powerful and resilient foundation upon which to build any system. Our current educational environment has endured so long in the midst of a tremendously changed society because its goals—uniformity, central control, and insulation from popular accountability—are all reinforced by the specific modes of organization we discussed in Section One. To achieve real change, we must replace the goals, tools, and habits of organization of our current system with those that support and embody our new priorities, which must in turn reflect the evolution of society over these past one hundred and fifty years.

Our plan for Multiple National Curricula does just this. It is a tool for gathering extensive information on what works in education and what doesn't. An educational system is, among other things, a technology for the transmission of knowledge, skills, and values. The Multiple National Curricula plan can provide information about what works without imposing an agenda of its own on those who make use of it. The data it will yield can be used to support any number of differing political, ideological, or pedagogical assertions. Our plan doesn't care what flag you fly, any more than an oven cares what you bake in it.

While useful tools like this are much needed, we wrote this plan because we also have structural goals for public schools, a wish for them to seek different outcomes than those they have historically embraced. These goals can be summed up in three words: responsiveness, achievement, and equity. We want schools that can improve themselves and can adapt to changing times, that can be reliably assessed, that have learning as a core value, and that have a fighting chance of providing equal educational opportunity to all students, even if that means treating them differently based on their differing needs.

There is a great deal of virtue in small answers as well. Small answers are those that grow up locally in response to local needs rather than descending from the clouds or bullying the townspeople like an occupying army. What we like perhaps best of all about our plan is that it encourages small answers by developing incentives and support systems that promote their adoption. It opens up the process of educational decision-making and curriculum development to those who have not before played significant roles—parents, teachers, and community groups, and it provides mechanisms to verify and disseminate the results of these new programs.

The Best Bet

We recognize that many, many people have their own thoughts on how to improve American education, and we are not so arrogant as to think we have the only Big Answer. However, we may have the only Big Answer that has a chance of living beyond its pages.

Most of the new ideas circulating around school reform—and there are many good ones—make more sense when linked to our proposal. School choice, whether you are for or against it, certainly makes more sense if there is a reasonable way to judge schools. Some, like merit pay and alternative teacher recruitment programs like Teach for America, make sense only if you can judge the performance of some teachers versus others. Debates over how school financing and privatization are linked to educational outcome become more rational and less ideological when there is solid data to back up the assertions. Good ideas like those of the Coalition for Essential Schools will propagate faster if their outcomes are verifiable and schools are free to adopt them.

The Multiple National Curricula proposal is nonideological and non-partisan. Like any plan for school improvement, however, it necessarily reflects a set of values and assumptions. It postulates that it is better to have more choices than fewer; that there is no "one best system" of public education or "one best curriculum" for everyone; that people of all backgrounds can learn to make responsible use of information if they have supportive mechanisms for them to do so; that we have the right and the duty to hold schools, teachers, and students accountable for learning.

Perhaps most centrally and most controversially, our proposal assumes that neither the government, nor the single school, nor the individual family is independently capable of determining what works best for a particular learning situation. Linked together, however, the combined "meta–intelligence" formed from thousands of experiences, thousands of decisions, and a variety of institutional perspectives can point to a range of best practices. We believe the autonomy, the innovation, and the rigor that the Multiple National Curricula plan encourages will produce outcomes for students and society that are both admirable in themselves and excellent points of departure for future exploration.

N O T E S

Chapter 1:

1. Berliner, D. 1993. Educational reform in an era of disinformation. *Education Policy Analysis Archives* 1(2). Education Policy Analysis Archives operates as an Internet LISTSERV under the name EDPLOYAR@ASUVM.INRE.ASU.EDU. Archives are accessible at http://info.asu.edu/asu-cwis/epaa/welcome.html.

2. Huelskamp, R.M. The Sandia report on education. *Phi Delta Kappan*, May 1993. See also *CENSORED: The news that didn't make the news and why. The 1994 Censored Yearbook* (1994). New York: Four Walls Eight Windows. Project Censored can also be reached at http://zippy.sonoma.edu:70/1/ ProjectCensored.

3. Whittington, D. 1991. What have seventeen-year-olds known in the past? *American Educational Research Journal* 28(4): 759-780.

4. U.S. Department of Education. National Center for Education Statistics. *Public and private elementary and secondary education statistics: School year 1991-92.*

5. Reaves, G. The U.S. is killing its young. U.N. says U.S. dangerous for children. *Dallas Morning News*, 25 Sept. 1993

6. Hanushek, E. A. 1989. The impact of differential expenditures on school performance. *Educational Researcher* 18(4): 45-62.

Chapter 2:

1. Tyack, D. B. 1974. *The one best system: A history of American urban education.* Cambridge: Harvard.

2. Nasaw, D. 1979. *Schooled to order: A social history of schooling in the United States.* New York: Oxford.

3. Hodas, S. (In Press). Technology refusal and the organizational culture of schools. In R. Kling (Ed.), *Computerization and Controversy.* Academic Press.

4. U.S. Department Of Education. National Center For Education Statistics. *Public school education financing for school year 1989-90.*

Chapter 3:

1. Valueline, 1993.

2. Tyson-Bernstein, H. and Woodward, A. Nineteenth-century policies for twenty-first century practice: The textbook reform dilemma. In Elliot, D. & Woodward, R. eds. (1990). *Textbooks and schooling in the United States.* Chicago: University of Chicago.

Chapter 4:

1. FairTest. 1990. *Fallout from the testing explosion: How 100 million standardized exams undermine equity and excellence in America's public schools* (3rd Edition).

2. Lofty, John S. 1993. Can Britain's national curriculum show America the way? *Educational Leadership* 50(5): 52-55.

3. Popham, W. James. 1991. *Appropriateness of Teachers' Test–Preparation Practices.* Presented at the Annual Meeting of the American Educational Research Association.

4. Gugliotta, Guy. Up in Arms About the 'American Experience'; History Curriculum Guidelines Play Down Traditional Heroes and Focus on Negatives, Critics Say. *Washington Post,* 28 Oct. 1994

5. Sanchez, Rene. History Curriculum Guides That Conservatives Criticized May Be Revised. *Washington Post,* 14 Jan. 1995

Chapter 7:

1. Rothfeder, J. 1992. *Privacy for sale: how computerization has made everyone's private life an open secret.* New York: Simon & Schuster.

2. Gandy, Oscar H. 1993. *The panoptic sort: A political economy of personal information.* Boulder: Westview.

Chapter 9:

1. Howley, A., Pendarvis, E., & Howley, C. (In Press). *Out of our heads: Anti–intellectualism in American schools.* New York: Teachers College.

2. U.S. Department Of Education. National Center For Education Statistics. *Characteristics of stayers, movers and leavers: Results from the teacher follow-up survey 1991-92.*

3. Choy, S., et al. 1993. *America's teachers: Profile of a profession.* A report prepared for the U.S. Department of Education, National Center for Education Statistics.

Chapter 10:

1. Friedman, M. 1962. *Capitalism and freedom.* Chicago: University of Chicago.